AGES
9+

GUINNESS WORLD RECORDS

AMAZING!
FUN FACTS & ACTIVITIES

AMERICAN
EDUCATION
PUBLISHING™

American Education Publishing™
An imprint of Carson-Dellosa Publishing LLC
Greensboro, North Carolina

Photo: Guinness World Records Limited

Photo: Guinness World Records Limited

WHAT'S INSIDE?

Photo: Guinness World Records Limited

CAUTION CAUTION CAUTIO

A Note to the Reader of This Book

Inside this book, you will find facts about unusual objects and creatures, epic journeys, and thrilling feats. Read and enjoy the stories, but never try to set a world record on your own! Breaking records can be dangerous and even life threatening. If you think you have a good idea for a safe, record-breaking event, talk to an adult. You can learn more about how to set a world record at guinnessworldrecords.com.

Throughout this book, you will find activity ideas that encourage you to learn more, get active, use your brain, be creative, and have fun. Try all the activities, but pause and think before you do each one. Ask yourself: What should I do to be safe and follow the rules? Do I need a parent's permission to go somewhere or to use materials? Always ask an adult if you are unsure.

Now, turn to any page. Get ready to be amazed by Guinness World Records® facts!

CAUTION CAUTION CAUTIO

Photo: Image used under license from Shutterstock, Inc.

STRANGE ANIMALS

Photo: Guinness World Records Limited

Smallest Dog Living (Height)

Photo: Guinness World Records Limited

Boo Boo, a long-haired Chihuahua, measured 4 in. (10.16 cm) tall on May 12, 2007. She lives in Raceland, Kentucky.

Did You Know?
Boo Boo was about the size of a thumb when she was born and was fed with an eyedropper every two hours.

ACTIVITIES

1. Boo Boo is four inches tall. What do you own that is about four inches tall? Use a ruler to find out.

   _____

2. Chihuahuas get their name from the Mexican state of Chihuahua. English has borrowed many words from Spanish. Can you fill in the English words?

Spanish		English
tornar ("to turn")	=	_____ ("a turning storm")
el lagarto ("the lizard")	=	_____ ("a large reptile")

Largest Rodent

The capybara has a head and body length of 3 ft. 3 in. (99.06 cm) and can weigh up to 174 lb. (79 kg). It is found in Argentina, Uruguay, and Brazil.

Did You Know?
Capybaras can be trained like dogs. A South American blind man trained a capybara as a guide animal.

Photo: Image used under license from Shutterstock, Inc.

ACTIVITIES

1. There are 16 ounces in a pound. How many ounces does a 174-pound capybara weigh?

   _____

2. A hamster weighs about five ounces. About how many hamsters would it take to weigh as much as a 174-pound capybara? Round to the nearest whole number.

   _____

3. Name two more rodents.

   _____   _____

Photo: Guinness World Records Limited

Nipper's Geronimo is an English lop. His ears measured 2 ft. 7 in. (79 cm) on November 1, 2003. He lived in Bakersfield, California.

Did You Know?
Rabbits can see who's behind them without turning their heads!

ACTIVITIES

1. How many more inches long would Nipper's Geronimo's ears need to be to measure one yard?

   _____

2. Would you rather have a rabbit with long ears, like the English lop, or a rabbit with short ears, like the mini rex? Explain your answer.

   _____

3. Give two synonyms for *rabbit*.

   _____   _____

Most Dogs Walked Simultaneously by an Individual

Photo: Guinness World Records Limited

Melissa Crispin Piche (Canada) walked 27 dogs at once on September 13, 2008, in Alberta, Canada.

Did You Know?
National Scoop the Poop week is held in April in the United States. In England, it is called *National Poop Scoop Week* and is held in July.

ACTIVITIES

1. List three things you can do simultaneously.

   _____   _____   _____

2. How many groups of 3 are in 27?

   _____

3. What would be easier: Walking 27 dogs or petting 27 cats? Explain your answer.

   _____

Greatest Color Vision

Photo: Image used under license from Shutterstock, Inc.

The eyes of a Stomatopod crustacean, like this mantis shrimp, contain eight or more different types of color photoreceptors—six more than most mammals. This allows them to see many colors that are invisible to the human eye.

Did You Know?
A mantis shrimp can hit with the force of a bullet.

CHECK THIS OUT!

The mantis shrimp has a powerful body part—its eyes. The mantis shrimp holds the Guinness World Record for the Greatest Color Vision. Its eyes have eight receptors, or color-sensing parts of the eyes. These receptors can sense colors that are invisible to other animals.

Humans' eyes have three receptors that can see about 10,000 colors. Dogs' eyes only have two receptors, and they cannot see some colors that humans can. With its eight color-sensing receptors, the mantis shrimp sees 10 times more colors than we do!

Another sea animal with amazing vision is the swordfish. Swordfish hold the world record for Hottest Fish Eyes. A swordfish can heat its eyeballs to as much as 82°F!

ACTIVITIES

1. About how many colors can the mantis shrimp see? Explain how you determined your answer.

_____

_____

2. Finish the sentence.

_____ have $\frac{1}{4}$ as many color receptors
as the mantis shrimp.

3. Which Celsius temperature is equal to the temperature that the swordfish can heat its eyes up to?

   a. 0°C

   b. 28°C

   c. 82°C

   d. 100°C

4. Fill in the table with information you read on page 10. If the information cannot be determined from the passage, write N/A.

Animal	Number of Receptors	Colors That Are Visible
Humans	3	
Dogs		
Mantis Shrimp		

5. Look around your room. How many different colors can you see? Circle your answer.

   more than 50   less than 50

6. With an adult, find several different shades of paint. Mix two paint colors together to form new colors. Give each new color you create a name. List them here.

_____   _____

_____   _____

Fastest Eater (Mammals)

Photo: Gary Meszaros/Photo Researchers, Inc.

The star-nosed mole can identify food, capture it, and eat it in an average "handling time" of 230 milliseconds, with the fastest time being 120 milliseconds.

Did You Know?

The star-nosed mole has 22 pink tentacles that form the star on its nose. Its tentacles can also detect food under water.

ACTIVITIES

1. There are 1,000 milliseconds in one second. It takes you about 100 milliseconds to blink. About how many times could you blink in the time it takes an average star-nosed mole to eat?

   _____

2. Most living creatures have the same number of body parts on each side. This is called *bilateral symmetry*. Due to this quality, how many tentacles does the star-nosed mole have on each side of its amazing nose?

   _____

Most Celebrated Canine Rescuer

Photo: Hans Reinhard/Photo Researchers, Inc.

Barry, a St. Bernard canine rescuer that lived from 1800 to 1814, rescued more than 40 people during his 12-year career on the Swiss Alps.

Did You Know?
Before these dogs became known as St. Bernards, they were called *Barry Dogs* or *Noble Steeds*.

ACTIVITIES

1. Barry rescued about 40 people in 12 years. About how many people did he rescue each year? Round to the nearest whole number.

   _____

2. Swiss people come from what country? Research to find out.

   _____

3. Has a dog ever helped you? Write about it.

   _____

   _____

Most Fearless Mammal

The honey badger will defend itself against animals of any size. Its skin is so tough that it is not hurt by bee stings, porcupine quills, or most snakebites. Its skin is also so loose that if a creature holds it by the scruff of the neck, it can turn inside its skin and bite the attacker until released.

Photo: Image used under license from Shutterstock, Inc.

Did You Know?
When a honey badger is frightened, it drops a "stink bomb" almost as smelly as a skunk's spray.

ACTIVITIES

1. The honey badger has super tough skin. What super tough body part would you like to have?

_____

2. The honey badger is the Most Fearless Mammal. Do you think any human or creature is truly fearless? Explain your answer.

_____

_____

_____

Longest Rabbit

Photo: Guinness World Records Limited

Darius, a Flemish giant rabbit, measured 4 ft. 3 in. (1.29 m) on April 6, 2010. He lives with his owner, Anette Edwards, in the United Kingdom.

Did You Know?

Rabbits have 18 toenails—four on each of their back feet and five on each of their front feet.

ACTIVITIES

1. Are you longer or shorter than Darius? Circle your answer.

   longer   **shorter**

2. What is the difference in inches between Darius's length and your length?

   _____

3. Where would a giant rabbit sleep at your house?

   _____

   _____

15

Slowest Fish

Photo: Digital Vision

Seahorses probably never attain speeds of more than 0.01 mph (0.016 km/h). They can't swim against the current and must hang on to coral and marine plants with their tails to avoid being swept away.

Did You Know?

Seahorses are the only species where the male carries the unborn babies in a special pouch in his abdomen.

CHECK THIS OUT!

Mysterious sea creatures have always captured people's imaginations. Children's books are full of stories about mermaids and seahorses. Unlike mermaids, however, seahorses are real.

Seahorses are unusual animals. They have heads like horses, pouches like kangaroos, and tails like monkeys. More than 30 different kinds of seahorses exist. They can range in size from one quarter of an inch to one foot long. Seahorses come in many colors. Some even use camouflage to hide from their enemies!

Seahorses are unusual because they mate for life. They are one of few fish species in which the male gives birth to the young. Babies are born as fully formed tiny seahorses. They immediately begin swimming in the ocean.

1. Mermaids are real creatures. True or false? Circle your answer.

true   **false**

2. An animal that uses camouflage for defense

    a. hides behind large objects.

    b. blends in with its surroundings.

    c. shows its teeth or claws.

    d. has no protection against predators.

3. Do you think a seahorse is unusual? Explain why or why not.

_____

_____

4. Name one way seahorses are like other fish.

_____

5. About how many varieties of seahorses exist?

    a. 50

    b. 25

    c. 30

    d. 45

6. Design a machine that could help seahorses swim faster. Draw it here and explain to a friend how it works.

Most Steps Walked Down by a Dog Facing Forwards Balancing a Glass of Water

Photo: Guinness World Records Limited

Sweet Pea, an Australian shepherd/border collie mix, walked down 10 steps while balancing a glass of water on her snout on January 5, 2008.

Did You Know?
There are about 400 million dogs in the world.

ACTIVITIES

1. If Sweet Pea performed her trick 30 times, how many steps would she walk down altogether?

   _____

2. Australian shepherds were bred to herd sheep. What other jobs do dogs perform for people?

   _____

3. Why are Australian shepherds called *Aussies*?

   _____

Largest Carnivore on Land

Photo: Guinness World Records Limited

Adult male polar bears weigh about 880–1,320 lb. (400–600 kg). They measure 7 ft. 10 in. to 8 ft. 6 in. (2.4–2.6 m) from nose to tail.

Did You Know?

Polar bears sometimes cover their black noses with their white paws so seals will not see them.

ACTIVITIES

1. Polar bears live along the Arctic Ocean. Describe the position of the Arctic Ocean on planet Earth.

   _____

2. Would eight 150-pound human adults weigh more or less than the largest polar bear? Circle your answer.

   more   **less**

3. What type of bear lives closest to your home?

   _____

Fish With the Largest Repertoire of Tricks

Photo: Guinness World Records Limited

As of October 2005, Albert Einstein, a calico fantail goldfish, could perform six tricks, including playing football and fetch. Albert was trained at the "Fish School" in Gibsonia, Pennsylvania.

Did You Know?

Another goldfish is in training to beat Albert Einstein's record. Comet plays basketball and soccer, swims through hoops, and has mastered other tricks.

ACTIVITIES

1. Invent a new trick a fish might learn to do.

   _____

2. A *repertoire* is a performer's list of practiced skills or abilities. Do you have a repertoire of skills in sports, music, art, or schoolwork? List three skills you have practiced extensively.

   _____

   _____

   _____

Smallest Living Horse

Photo: Guinness World Records Limited

Thumbelina, a miniature sorrel brown mare, measures 17.5 in. (44.5 cm) tall and weighs 71 lb. (32.3 kg). She lives in St. Louis, Missouri.

Did You Know?

Thumbelina is a small horse with a big heart. Every year, she visits needy, abused, and disabled children in her Thumby-mobile.

ACTIVITIES

1. Use paper, blocks, or other materials to make a model of a horse that is 17.5 inches tall. Write about what you did.

   _____

2. Measure the distance from the floor to your knees. What is the difference in inches between that height and Thumbelina's height?

   _____

3. Would you rather have a large horse or a tiny horse? Explain your answer.

   _____

Tallest Living Horse

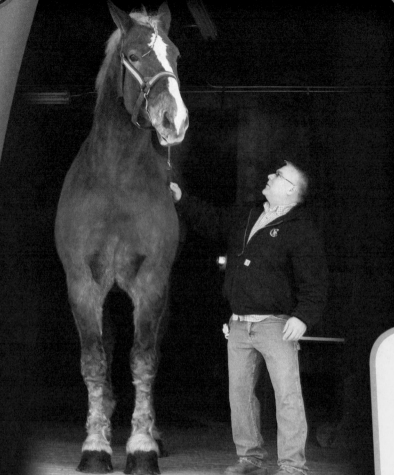

Photo: Guinness World Records Limited

Big Jake measured
6 ft. 10.7 in. (2.101 m)
tall, without shoes,
on January 19, 2010.
He lives in Poynette,
Wisconsin.

Did You Know?

Horses are able to stand while sleeping without falling down.

CHECK THIS OUT!

Many people know that a horse is a tall animal. But, this Belgian gelding raises the standard even higher.

Big Jake measured 20 hands, 2.75 inches high without shoes. Big Jake was measured three times with the same measurement recorded each time. He is owned by Smokey Hollow Farms in Poynette, Wisconsin.

The record for Tallest Mule belongs to Apollo. His height was recorded at 19 hands.

Horses and mules are measured in units called *hands*. Each hand is about four inches. A horse is measured from the ground to the highest point of its withers (shoulders). Most horses are about 16 hands high.

ACTIVITIES

1. How many hands equal one foot?

_____

2. In inches, how much taller is Big Jake than most horses?

_____

3. About how tall is Big Jake in feet and inches?

   a. 5 feet, 11 inches

   b. 6 feet, 11 inches

   c. 7 feet, 6 inches

   d. 6 feet, 2 inches

4. What is your height in feet and inches? How many hands tall are you?

_____

_____

5. The Tallest Ox measured 6 feet, 8 inches tall. The Tallest Mammal, a giraffe, was 19 feet tall. Order the record-setting animals from *1* to *4*, with *1* being shortest and *4* being tallest.

   _____ **horse**

   _____ **mule**

   _____ **giraffe**

   _____ **ox**

6. If a giraffe were measured in hands, how many hands tall would the Tallest Giraffe be?

_____

Striker rolled down a non-electric car window in 11.34 seconds on September 1, 2004, in Quebec City, Quebec, Canada.

Photo: Guinness World Records Limited

Did You Know?
Dogs can understand 150 to 200 words. They are especially good at understanding hand signals.

ACTIVITIES

1. What can you do in about 11 seconds? Can you put on a jacket and zip it up? Send a text or e-mail? Write what you can do in that time.

_____

2. How many seconds does it take you to open a window at your home? Have a friend time you.

_____

3. Why might a dog want to open a car window?

_____

Most Dolphins Born in a Year

Photo: ©2004 Brand X Pictures

Eleven dolphins were born between January 28 and December 4, 2008, at Delphinus Xcaret in Riviera Maya, Quintana Roo, Mexico.

Did You Know?
Dolphins do not chew their food. They swallow it whole!

ACTIVITIES

1. How many young dolphins would there be if one dolphin were born each month for two years?

   _____

2. Write the months of the year that contain the letter *y*.

   _____   _____

   _____   _____

3. If you were a dolphin, how would you celebrate your birthday?

   _____

Heaviest Spider

Photo: Guinness World Records Limited

Rosi, a female Goliath bird-eating spider, weighed 6.17 oz. (175 g) on July 27, 2007. She lives in Andorf, Austria.

Did You Know?
The Goliath bird-eating spider does not have teeth, but uses its large, inch-long fangs to bite.

ACTIVITIES

1. Does Rosi weigh more or less than one-half pound? Circle your answer.

   more   **less**

2. What do most spiders eat?

   _____

3. Who is Goliath? Why is Rosi's breed of spider called *Goliath*?

   _____

   _____

Most Tennis Balls Held in the Mouth by a Dog

Photo: Guinness World Records Limited

Augie, a golden retriever, held five regulation-sized tennis balls in his mouth on July 6, 2003. He lived in Dallas, Texas.

Did You Know?

Golden retrievers make good service dogs. Service dogs guide blind people, pull wheelchairs, and turn on lights. Some can dial 9-1-1.

ACTIVITIES

1. Estimate how many books, toys, or other items will fit in your backpack. Test your hypothesis. How close was your guess?

   _____

2. How many balls would Augie hold in his mouth if he did his trick each day for one week?

   _____

3. Why do you think Augie likes tennis balls?

   _____

Largest Lizard

Photo: Image used under license from Shutterstock, Inc.

Adult male Komodo dragons are 7 ft. 5 in. (2.25 m) in length and weigh 130 lb. (59 kg).

Did You Know?

The saliva in the Komodo dragon's mouth has over 50 kinds of bacteria. Most animals die of blood poisoning within 24 hours of being bitten.

CHECK THIS OUT!

When you hear of dragons, you may think of fictional beasts that breathe fire. But did you know that a lizard called a *Komodo dragon* exists that is just as fierce? These lizards have been alive for millions of years, but their existence was a mystery until about 100 years ago.

The Komodo's teeth are often compared to those of a shark. A Komodo has about 60 teeth, which are broken and replaced frequently. This keeps the teeth sharp. The dragons use their sharp sense of smell to find prey.

Komodo dragons are also scavengers and eat the bodies of dead animals. They can eat up to 80 percent of their body weight in one meal. If you weighed 100 pounds, that would mean you would have to eat an 80-pound hamburger to keep up with this dragon!

ACTIVITIES

1. In what way are Komodo dragons and sharks alike?

   a. They both climb trees.

   b. They both use gills to breathe.

   c. They both have teeth that are replaced often.

   d. They are gray in color.

2. People have known about Komodo dragons for millions of years. True or false? Circle your answer.

   true   **false**

3. How does the Komodo dragon compare with your idea of dragons from fictional tales? Fill in the Venn diagram to compare and contrast the two creatures.

Komodo Dragons   **Fictional Dragons**

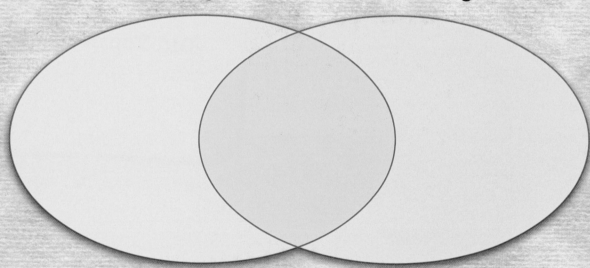

4. From the passage on page 28, you can conclude that Komodo dragons are

   a. dangerous animals.

   b. slow, lazy creatures.

   c. related to dinosaurs.

   d. small.

5. The dragons use their sharp sense of smell to find prey. What is a synonym for *sharp*?

Highest Ranking Camel

Photo: Guinness World Records Limited

Bert was accepted as a Reserve Duty Sheriff for the Los Angeles County Sheriff's Department of San Dimas, California, on April 5, 2003.

Did You Know?
Camels don't really spit; they throw up!

ACTIVITIES

Write a story about a sheriff, a camel, and a mystery that needs to be solved.

_____

_____

_____

_____

_____

_____

Highest Jump by a Dog

Cinderella May A Holly Grey jumped 5 ft. 8 in. (1.72 m) high on October 7, 2006.

Photo: Guinness World Records Limited

Did You Know?

Pictures of greyhounds were carved in Egyptian tombs dating as far back as 5,000 years ago.

ACTIVITIES

1. Have a friend hold a yardstick or tape measure while you jump beside it. How high did you jump?

   _____

2. Some organizations help greyhounds who are former racing dogs that are no longer wanted. What is the name of an organization near you that helps animals? Research to find out.

   _____

3. What name would you give to a high-jumping dog?

   _____

Photo: Thomas & Pat Leeson/Photo Researchers, Inc.

A colony of black-tailed prairie dogs, discovered in 1901, contained about 400 million residents. The "town" covered about 23,706 sq. mi. (61,400 km²), almost the size of Ireland.

Did You Know?

Prairie dogs seem to kiss each other when they meet, although they're really just touching their teeth together.

ACTIVITIES

1. A square mile is an area of land shaped like a square. How many feet long is a square mile on each of its four sides?

   _____

2. Prairie dogs live underground in connected tunnels. Draw a prairie dog town.

Largest Horn Circumference on a Steer

Photo: Guinness World Records Limited

Lurch's horns measured 37.5 in. (95.25 cm) in circumference on May 6, 2003. His horn span was about 6 ft. 10.6 in. (2.1 m) long. Lurch is an African Watusi steer and lives in Gassville, Arkansas.

Did You Know?

Ofelia, a longhorn steer, lives on President George W. Bush's ranch with her calves Ellie and Logan. All were named after former staff members.

ACTIVITIES

1. Circumference measures the distance around a circle. What is the circumference of your wrist in inches? Use a tape measure to find out.

   _____

2. Measure this line in inches.

   _____ _____ **inches**

3. If the line you measured became a circle, what would be its circumference?

   _____

Smallest Police Dog

Photo: Guinness World Records Limited

Midge, a Chihuahua/rat terrier mix, measures 11 in. (28 cm) tall, 23 in. (58 cm) long, and weighs 8 lb. (3.6 kg). She works as an official Law Enforcement Work Dog at the Geauga County Sheriff's Office in Chardon, Ohio.

Did You Know?

Sheriff McClelland takes police dog Midge with him everywhere. She even has her own pair of goggles for rides on the sheriff's motorcycle.

CHECK THIS OUT!

When you think of police dogs, you may think of German shepherds. But, the world's Smallest Police Dog is a cross between a Chihuahua and rat terrier. Her name is Midge, and she is only 11 inches tall and 23 inches long. That includes her 7-inch tail!

Midge may not look like a police dog, but she is an official K9. She is trained to sniff out drugs. She is small enough to search in cars and school lockers.

Midge lives and works with her owner, Sheriff Dan McClelland, in Chardon, Ohio. Midge was born on November 6, 2005, and passed the police dog test just one year later. Midge may not be a big dog, but she has a big job!

1. How old will Midge be in 2015?

   _____

2. Midge's tail is about what fraction of the length of her body?

   a. $\frac{1}{2}$ of her body

   b. $\frac{1}{4}$ of her body

   c. $\frac{1}{3}$ of her body

   d. $\frac{3}{4}$ of her body

3. Using a ruler, draw a picture of Midge to scale. Use this scale: $\frac{1}{16}$ of an inch equals one inch.

4. What are two ways that Midge's size helps her to sniff out drugs?

   1. _____

   2. _____

5. The Most Successful Sniffer Dog is Snag, a Labrador retriever. He has made 118 drug recoveries with a total cost of $810,000,000. What is $810,000,000 divided by 118? Round your answer to the nearest hundredth.

   _____

6. What is the capital of Ohio? How many other cities can you name that begin with the same letter as Ohio's capital?

   _____

   _____

Photo: Digital Vision

Lonesome George is the only living Abingdon Island giant tortoise. He currently lives at the Charles Darwin Research Center on the Galapagos Islands, Ecuador.

Did You Know?

The leatherback sea turtle can grow to be 8 ft. (2.44 m) long and can weigh 1,500 lb. (680 kg). That is as much as a full-grown moose.

ACTIVITIES

1. Over 16,000 species are endangered. Some are listed below. Circle one species you know. Star one species you would like to learn about.

angel shark	California tiger salamander
black-footed ferret	loggerhead sea turtle
callippe silverspot butterfly	Asian elephant

2. Reasons that animals are endangered include pollution, loss of habitat, and hunting. Name one thing humans can do to help protect animals.

Longest Tongue on a Dog

Photo: Guinness World Records Limited

Puggy, a Pekingese, has a tongue that measured 4.5 in. (11.43 cm) on May 8, 2009. Puggy lives in Bedford, Texas.

Did You Know?

Dog nose prints are unique and can identify a dog like fingerprints can identify a human.

ACTIVITIES

1. How long is your tongue? Use a ruler to find out.

   _____

2. Write the length of Puggy's tongue as a fraction.

   _____

3. The Pekingese is a small, muscular dog with shaggy fur and a proud personality. Describe your pet or a pet you would like to have.

   _____

Oldest Kinkajou in Captivity

Photo: Guinness World Records Limited

Huggy Bear was 27 years and 6 months old in January 2004. He lives in Holiday, Florida.

Did You Know?
Kinkajous are sometimes called *honey bears* because they raid bees' nests. They slurp the honey with long, skinny tongues.

ACTIVITIES

1. Huggy Bear was 27 in 2004. In what year will he be 40?

   _____

2. In what year will you be 20 years old?

   _____

3. Unlike wild animals, animals in captivity live with humans. List some places you might find wild and captive animals.

   wild animals: _____

   captive animals: _____

Tallest Living Dog (Ever)

Photo: Guinness World Records Limited

Giant George, a Great Dane, measured 3 ft. 7 in. (1.092 m) tall on February 15, 2010. He lives in Tucson, Arizona.

Did You Know?
Great Danes often double in size between one and two months of age.

ACTIVITIES

1. Are you taller or shorter than Giant George? Circle your answer.

   taller   **shorter**

2. What could Giant George do that smaller dogs cannot?

   _____

3. What could small dogs do that Giant George cannot?

   _____

Noisiest Land Animal

Photo: ©Mark Bowler/naturepl.com

In full voice, the howler monkey can be heard clearly up to 3 mi. (4.8 km) away. The shrill screams have been described as a cross between the bark of a dog and the bray of a donkey, increased a thousandfold.

Did You Know?

Despite how loud howler monkeys are, it can be hard to spot them because they hang out in the treetops so they can eat younger, greener leaves.

CHECK THIS OUT!

Animals that live in the rainforest have their own special alarm clocks—howler monkeys! These monkeys make loud, wailing noises at dawn and dusk. Their howls can be heard three to four miles into the forest.

Male howler monkeys are black. Females are brown. As adults, both males and females weigh about 15 pounds and grow to be about two feet long. This does not include their 30-inch prehensile tail. A prehensile tail is often used for grabbing things and is commonly used for balance. Because howler monkeys are herbivores, their diet includes mostly leaves, fruit, and flowers.

Howler monkeys are hunted for food by local tribes. Some are even exported as pets. Scientists are concerned that, without more awareness, howler monkeys will become extinct during our lifetime.

ACTIVITIES

1. How far can the calls of howler monkeys be heard?

   _____

2. What is a *prehensile tail*? Can you name other animals with prehensile tails?

   _____

   _____

3. How would you compare male and female howler monkeys?

   a. Both are the same color, size, and weight.

   b. Both are the same color and size but different weights.

   c. Both are the same size and weight but different colors.

   d. Both are the same size, but different weights and colors.

4. Exotic animals should not be sold as pets. Explain why you agree or disagree.

   _____

   _____

   _____

5. Howler monkeys are herbivores. What does this mean? What other animals do you know that are herbivores?

   _____

   _____

6. Unscramble words you read on page 40.

   erfarnstio   _____

   ehrlow knomyse   _____

   irebvesorh   _____

   eheepslirn itla   _____

Highest Jump by a Pig

Photo: Guinness World Records Limited

Kotetsu, a potbellied pig, jumped 2 ft. 3.5 in. (70 cm) high on August 22, 2004, at a farm in Mie, Japan.

Did You Know?
Potbellied pigs rarely weigh over 150 lb. (68 kg). They are popular pets because they are smaller than farm pigs and can be housebroken.

ACTIVITIES

1. Kotetsu jumped 2 feet, 3.5 inches. How many inches is that in all?

   _____

2. Use tape to mark a start line on the floor and a finish line two feet, four inches away. How many hops or jumps does it take you to get from one line to the other?

   _____

3. Would you like a pig for a pet? Explain your answer.

   _____

Slowest Mammal

Photo: Digital Vision

The three-toed sloth's ground speed averages 6–8 ft. (1.8–2.4 m) per minute. In trees, it moves at nearly double that rate, traveling an average of 15 ft. (4.6 m) per minute.

Did You Know?

The sloth's curved claws allow it to hang upside down in trees while it sleeps.

ACTIVITIES

1. Why do you think the three-toed sloth can move faster in trees than on land?

   _____

2. Have a slow-motion contest with a friend as you go down the stairs, eat a snack, or tie your shoes. Who was slowest?

   _____

3. What time of day do you move slowest? Fastest?

   _____

Hungriest Bear Species

Photo: Digital Vision

In order to survive, a giant panda must eat 38 percent of its weight in bamboo shoots or 15 percent of its weight in bamboo leaves and stems each day. It spends up to 15 hours per day eating.

Did You Know?
Giant pandas are a national treasure in China and are protected by law. The Chinese call them *large bear-cats*.

ACTIVITIES

Write your weight in the boxes.

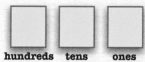

hundreds   tens   ones

Now, write your weight again the same way. See the decimal point? This number is 10% of your weight.

Challenge: What is 15% of your weight? Would you like to eat that many pounds of leaves each day?

Most Expensive Painting by Elephants

Photo: Guinness World Records Limited

The painting sold for $39,000 in Thailand on February 19, 2005. The painting is titled *Cold Wind, Swirling Mist, Charming Lanna I.*

Did You Know?
An elephant has four molars, one on the top and bottom of each side of its mouth. A single molar is about the size of a brick.

(ACTIVITIES)

1. What number is in the ten-thousands place in 39,000?

_____

2. What would you buy with $39,000?

_____

3. Why do you think someone would spend a large sum of money on a one-of-a-kind artwork?

_____

Largest Domestic Goat Horns

Photo: Guinness World Records Limited

Uncle Sam's horns measured 4 ft. 4 in. (1.32 m) tip to tip on April 16, 2004, in Rothsville, Pennsylvania.

Did You Know?

A goat's horns grow throughout its entire life. A growth ring is added each year. By counting its rings, you can determine a goat's age.

CHECK THIS OUT!

These record-setting horns are long—really long. A goat named *Uncle Sam* set the Guinness World Record for the Longest Domestic Goat Horns. His horns spanned 52 inches from tip to tip!

Uncle Sam was owned by Bill and Vivian Wentling and lived on a farm in Rothsville, Pennsylvania. Uncle Sam's horns were so long that they had a slight curl. His left horn measured 39.33 inches, and his right horn measured 40.12 inches.

There are plenty of other animals out there with long horns. The Longest Bull Horns each measured 4 feet, 7 inches and belonged to a bull named *Gopal*. The Longest Horns of any living animal belong to an Asian water buffalo. The horns of one buffalo measured 13 feet, 10 inches from tip to tip.

ACTIVITIES

1. What is the difference in feet and inches between Uncle Sam's horn span and someone who is six feet tall?

   a. 1 foot, 8 inches

   b. 2 feet, 4 inches

   c. 4 feet, 1 inch

   d. 4 feet, 4 inches

2. Circle five words you read on page 46 to complete the word search. Use the word bank to help you.

   Uncle Sam   goat   bull   buffalo   horns

S	T	V	B	R	C	C	R
D	H	O	R	N	S	Y	P
G	B	U	F	F	A	L	O
Y	B	T	B	B	L	L	S
G	L	U	U	G	O	A	T
Z	M	H	L	C	V	H	Z
U	N	C	L	E	S	A	M
D	D	H	P	S	Y	S	O

3. How much longer is the horn span from tip to tip of the Asian water buffalo than the horn span of Uncle Sam?

   _____

4. What is the total length, in inches, of Uncle Sam's left and right horns? Circle your answer.

   more than 80 inches   **less than 80 inches**

5. Write <, >, or = to complete the equation.

   4 feet, 7 inches   ◯   52 inches

Largest Tree-Dwelling Mammal

Photo: Digital Vision

Orangutan adult males weigh approximately 183 lb. (83 kg) and measure 5 ft. (1.5 m) tall. They have an arm span of approximately 6 ft. 6 in. (2 m).

Did You Know?

After watching villagers take a boat across water, orangutans have been known to untie and ride the boat on their own.

ACTIVITIES

1. Measure a length of yarn or string six feet, six inches long. Wrap it around things inside and outside. What things could an adult male orangutan reach around with arms that long?

   _____

2. Are you taller or shorter than an adult male orangutan? Circle your answer.

   taller   **shorter**

3. What do you think orangutans see from the treetops?

   _____

Longest Goldfish

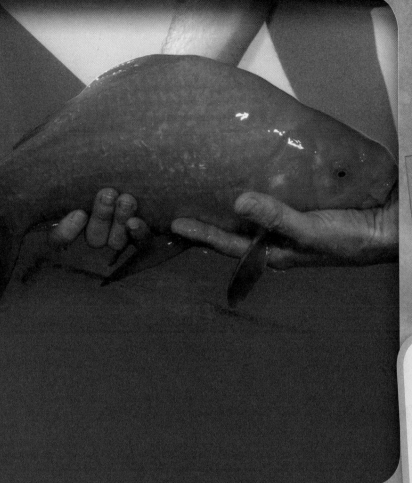

Photo: Guinness World Records Limited

The world's longest goldfish measures 18.7 in. (47.4 cm) from snout to tail fin. The measurement was taken on March 24, 2003, in Hapert, Netherlands.

Did You Know?

Goldfish will turn gray if they are kept in the dark for too long.

ACTIVITIES

Some goldfish are large and some are tiny. Some have dark spots or golden flecks. Draw a goldfish in the bowl.

Strangest Animal Diet

Photo: Digital Vision

An internal examination of an ostrich that had been living at London Zoo (UK) revealed that during its life, it had swallowed (among other things) an alarm clock, three coins, a roll of film, three gloves, a handkerchief, and a pencil.

Did You Know?

Asian moths are known to drink the tears of wild cows, buffalo, and elephants—right from their eyelids!

ACTIVITIES

1. Where do you think the alarm clock and the other strange objects came from?

   _____

2. What is the strangest thing you have ever eaten?

   _____

3. Name one thing you can do to keep animals healthy and safe at your house, at the zoo, or in the wild.

   _____

Longest Species of Beetle

Photo: Patrick Landmann/Photo Researchers, Inc.

The Titan beetle is found in South America. Its body measures 5.9 in. (15 cm) long.

Did You Know?
Titan beetles have to launch themselves from trees because they are too heavy to take off from the ground!

ACTIVITIES

1. How many inches long is your hand?

   _____

2. In ancient Greek mythology, the Titans were giants who were overthrown by the Olympians. Today, *titan* can mean "having gigantic size or power." Explain why these things are titan.

   Titan beetle: _____

   The ship *Titanic*: _____

   Saturn's moon Titan: _____

Fastest Time to Pop 100 Balloons by a Dog

Photo: ©2010 Michael A. Pliskin/pliskindesigns.com

Anastasia popped 100 balloons in 44.49 seconds on February 28, 2008. She lives in Southern California.

Did You Know?
Anastasia likes balloons so much, she gets excited even if a blimp flies over her yard!

CHECK THIS OUT!

Some dogs do not like loud noises, but Anastasia doesn't mind! Her owner first noticed Anastasia's special talent for popping balloons at a New Year's Eve party. When all of the balloons appeared, Anastasia wanted to bite as many as she could. Now, she holds the world record!

Her first balloon contest in 2005 involved helium balloons. Anastasia, a Jack Russell terrier, was one of 10 finalists in that contest. Now, she bites standard party balloons attached to the ground. Her world record is 100 balloons popped in 44.49 seconds.

Anastasia has shown her skills on several TV shows. In fact, Anastasia actually broke her old world record of 53.7 seconds on a national morning TV show.

ACTIVITIES

1. What adjective could best describe Anastasia?

   a. lonely

   b. heavy

   c. energetic

   d. bored

2. Finish the sentence.

   Anastasia pops balloons by _____.

3. Using only your hands, how many balloons can you pop in 60 seconds?

   _____

4. Why might helium-filled balloons be more difficult to use when breaking a world record?

   _____

   _____

5. Balloons can come in all different shapes and colors. Decorate these balloons any way you like.

Most Dangerous Lizard

Photo: Image used under license from Shutterstock, Inc.

A Gila monster carries enough venom in its lower jaw to kill two adult males. When it bites with its sharp, fragile teeth, it may hang on and actively chew for several minutes.

Did You Know?

A medication for type 2 diabetes is made from the Gila monster's saliva, and has been referred to as *lizard spit*.

ACTIVITIES

Gila (pronounced HEE-la) monsters have forked tongues and a snorting hiss. They are poisonous, but will attack only when disturbed. Few deaths have been reported as a result of a Gila monster. Do you think they deserve the name *monster*? Explain why or why not.

_____

_____

_____

_____

Largest Mouth of All Land Animals

Photo: ©2001 Corbis Corporation

The hippopotamus can open its jaws almost 180 degrees. In a fully grown male hippo, this equates to an average gape of 4 ft. (1.2 m).

Did You Know?

Hippo sweat looks like blood. But it is only a red mucus that keeps the hippo's skin from getting sunburned.

ACTIVITIES

1. A circle has 360°. A hippo can open its mouth almost 180°. That's half a circle! Color one-half of this circle.

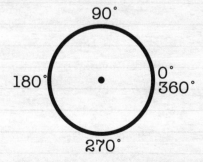

2. Which of the five vowels is not in the word *hippopotamus*?

_____

Fastest Ferret

Photo: Guinness World Records Limited

On July 11, 1999, Warhol, an albino ferret, ran 32 ft. 9 in. (10 m) in 12.59 seconds at the North of England Ferret Racing Championships. He lives with his owner in the United Kingdom.

Did You Know?
Ferrets have been used to carry television cables through pipes to help cable installers.

ACTIVITIES

1. Warhol kept his racing time under 13 seconds by what fraction of a second?

_____

2. Ferret owners call their pets *ferts*, *furballs*, and *carpet sharks*. What is a nickname for a pet you know?

_____

3. A group of ferrets is called a *business of ferrets*. Do you know another funny name for a group of animals?

_____

Most Skips by a Dog in One Minute

Photo: Guinness World Records Limited

Sweet Pea, an Australian shepherd/border collie mix, and her owner, Alex Rothaker (USA), skipped rope 75 times in one minute on August 8, 2007, in New York City, New York.

Did You Know?

It is unusual for a dog to jump rope, but Sweet Pea has learned many things. Sometimes, her friends jump rope with her.

ACTIVITIES

1. What favorite activity would you like a pet to do with you?

   _____

2. Sweet Pea skipped 75 times in one minute. How many times could she jump in five minutes?

   _____

3. If a dog skips 260 times in four minutes, how many skips are done each minute?

   _____

Largest Snail

Photo: Guinness World Records Limited

An African giant snail measured 15.5 in. (39.3 cm) from snout to tail and weighed nearly 2 lb. (900 g). It was collected in Sierra Leone, Africa, in June 1976.

Did You Know?

African giant snails have huge appetites. They prefer fruits and vegetables, but may feast on tree bark and eat paint off houses.

CHECK THIS OUT!

You might expect a snail to set the record for the slowest animal in the world. So, you may be surprised to hear about Verne, the world's Fastest Land Snail. The snail completed a 12.2-inch course in exactly 2 minutes, 13 seconds. He traveled 0.09 inches per second. To put this into perspective, it would take Verne about eight days to travel one mile!

Another amazing snail set the record for being the world's Largest Snail. Named *Gee Geronimo*, it has held the record since June 1976. Gee Geronimo was an African giant snail. Although this type of snail looks like the common garden snail, the African giant snail is much bigger. The shell of most garden snails is only about 1.18 inches long, but the shell of an African giant snail can measure up to 10.75 inches long!

ACTIVITIES

1. How many years has Gee Geronimo held the record for the world's Largest Snail?

   _____

2. Estimate how fast you could travel one mile. Then, have a friend time you. Was your estimation correct?

   _____

3. What is the difference in length between the shell of an average garden snail and the shell of an average African giant snail?

   a. 9.93 inches

   b. 11.93 inches

   c. 9.63 inches

   d. 9.57 inches

4. Snails aren't the only animals that have shells. Circle the animals that have shells.

   turtles   **anteaters**

   crabs   **armadillos**

   rhinos   **elephants**

5. Estimate the weight of the common garden snail. Explain your thinking.

   _____

   _____

   _____

   _____

6. Would you like to have a pet snail? Explain why or why not.

   _____

   _____

Longest Tail on a Pony

Photo: Guinness World Records Limited

On March 28, 2008, Delies Babe Romper, a miniature stallion, had a tail that measured 8 ft. 6 in. (2.59 m) at a farm in Litchfield, Minnesota.

Did You Know?

Before a horse falls asleep on its feet, it locks its back legs so it will not fall over!

ACTIVITIES

1. What is the length of Delies Babe Romper's tail in inches?

_____

2. What animal would you like to own in a miniature version?

_____

3. How long is your hair? Use a ruler or tape measure to find out.

_____

Largest Millipede

Photo: Guinness World Records Limited

The largest millipede in the world is an African giant black millipede. It measures 15.2 in. (38.7 cm) in length, 2.6 in. (6.7 cm) in circumference, and has 256 legs.

Did You Know?

Millipedes breathe through small holes located on the sides of their bodies.

ACTIVITIES

1. The prefix *milli-* means "thousand." How do you think the millipede got its name?

   _____

2. Use paper, clay, or foil to make a model of a 15-inch-long millipede. Tell what you did.

   _____

3. How many legs does the African giant black millipede have on each side?

   _____

Tallest Mammal

Adult male giraffes measure between 15 and 18 ft. (4.6–5.5 m) tall. Giraffes are found in the dry savannah and open woodland areas of sub-Saharan Africa.

Did You Know?

A giraffe's tongue can grow to be 18–20 in. (46–51 cm) long, about as long as your arm.

Photo: ©2000 PhotoDisc, Inc.

ACTIVITIES

1. A one-story building is about 10 feet tall. About how many stories tall is a male giraffe?

   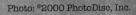

2. What would you do today if you were as tall as a giraffe?

   _____

3. The Sahara Desert divides the continent of Africa. Write the name of a country in sub-Saharan Africa.

   _____

Largest Egg From a Living Bird

Photo: Guinness World Records Limited

An ostrich laid an egg that weighed 5 lb. 11.32 oz. (2.589 kg). The measurement was taken on May 17, 2008, at a farm in Borlänge, Sweden.

Did You Know?

One ostrich egg is about as big as 24 chicken eggs and takes 40 days to hatch. It would take 40 minutes to hard-boil an ostrich egg.

ACTIVITIES

1. The largest egg was about 5 pounds, 11 ounces. How many more ounces would it need to weigh 6 pounds?

   _____

2. One ostrich egg could make eight pans of brownies or 12 servings of scrambled eggs. What dish would you make with an ostrich egg?

   _____

3. What is your favorite way to eat eggs?

   _____

63

Longest Ears on a Dog (Ever)

Photo: Guinness World Records Limited

Tigger's right ear measures 13.74 in. (34.9 cm) long, and his left ear measures 13.46 in. (34.2 cm) long. He lives in St. Joseph, Illinois.

Did You Know?
A dog's sense of smell is 1,000 times more sensitive than a human's.

ACTIVITIES

1. Have a friend trace your two feet on paper. How long is each one in inches? Are they exactly the same size? Measure to find out.

   _____

2. Think of a name for a superhero dog with super long ears.

   _____

3. How could your superhero dog help people?

   _____

Photo: Guinness World Records Limited

CRAZY CREATIONS

Photo: Guinness World Records Limited

Largest Bottle Cap Mosaic

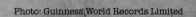

Photo: Guinness World Records Limited

A mosaic containing 3,614,468 bottle caps was made by students at the Freiherr vom Stein School in Hessisch Lichtenau, Germany, in 2010.

Did You Know?
The mosaic spelled out the school's initials.

ACTIVITIES

A mosaic is a picture that emerges from the arrangement of many tiny pieces. Color in circles to make a mosaic.

○○○○○○○○○○○
○○○○○○○○○○○
○○○○○○○○○○○
○○○○○○○○○○○
○○○○○○○○○○○
○○○○○○○○○○○

Largest Ice Cream Scoop Pyramid

Photo: Guinness World Records Limited

In Maui, Hawaii, on May 18, 2000, Baskin-Robbins International constructed a pyramid from 3,100 scoops of ice cream.

Did You Know?

The 21-layer pyramid stood for about 45 minutes before it began to melt.

ACTIVITIES

1. If $\frac{1}{10}$ of the scoops were strawberry, how many were some other flavor?

   _____

2. If each person ate 2.5 scoops, how many people could be served?

   _____

3. A pyramid is a three-dimensional shape. Circle other 3-D shapes.

cylinder	**circle**	**triangle**
sphere	**cube**	**square**

Largest Cardboard Box Sculpture

Photo: Guinness World Records Limited

In Cheney, Washington, in 2007, volunteers used cardboard boxes to build a 8,083.25-sq.-ft. (750.96-m²) replica of a medieval castle.

Did You Know?
The castle was 111 ft. 9 in. (34.06 m) long and 6 ft. 8 in. (2.03 m) tall.

ACTIVITIES

Check each feature you would include in a replica of a medieval castle.

- [ ] **great hall:** central inside area for daily business
- [ ] **gatehouse:** guarded entryway
- [ ] **moat:** ditch around perimeter
- [ ] **towers:** tall structures that provide defensive positions
- [ ] **keep:** safest, most heavily defended room
- [ ] **drawbridge:** retractable bridge
- [ ] **battlements:** defenses along the top wall

Most Henna Tattoos Completed in an Hour

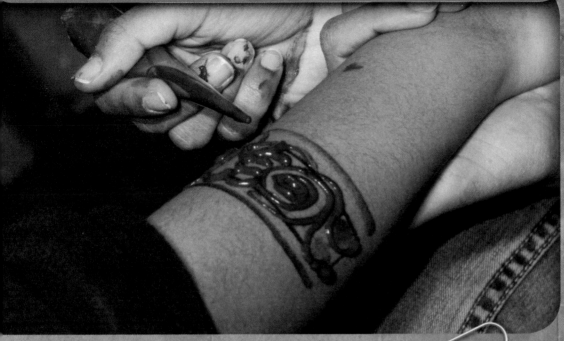

Photo: Guinness World Records Limited

Pavandeep Ahluwalia-Hundal (UK) completed 314 henna armband tattoos in one hour in Ilford, Essex, United Kingdom, on December 15, 2008.

Did You Know?
Henna is a brown, non-permanent dye used to stain intricate designs on the skin. The process is called *mendhi*.

ACTIVITIES

Mendhi artists use beautiful, detailed designs. Trace and color this mendhi design.

GUINNESS WORLD RECORDS™

Largest Toothpick Mosaic

飛夢
～輝ける未来へ～

Photo: Guinness World Records Limited

The largest toothpick mosaic was 436.16 sq. ft. (40.521 m^2) and was created by the students of Tsugeno High School (Japan). It was finished and presented on October 5, 2008.

Did You Know?
In the 17th century, toothpicks used by people in the upper class were made from gold, silver, or ivory.

CHECK THIS OUT!

When was the last time your whole school participated in the same event? Some schools host festivals or other events that raise money for charity. Some schools have sports matches or pep rallies in which everyone participates. Sometimes, even community members are invited to take part. These can be fun events for everyone involved.

At a high school in Japan, all 229 students of the school participated in something a little different. They set a Guinness World Record! The students worked together to create the world's Largest Toothpick Mosaic. The finished mosaic, which had an area of 436.16 square feet, was displayed in Aichi, Shinshiro City, Japan. The students at Tsugeno High School used a total of 1,620,840 toothpicks in seven different colors!

1. The area of this shape is 441 square feet. If each side is the same length, what is the length of each side?

$A = 441$ sq. ft.

$L =$ _____

2. Find several toothpicks. What interesting shape or design can you make using only toothpicks? Draw it here.

3. In what school-wide event have you participated?

_____

4. If toothpicks come in boxes of 100, how many boxes of toothpicks were needed for the mosaic? Round to the nearest tenth.

   a. 16,208.4 boxes

   b. 16,208 boxes

   c. 1,620.84 boxes

   d. 162,084 boxes

5. How many students would Tsugeno High School have if enrollment doubled? Circle your answer.

   more than 500   **less than 500**

Tallest Bottle Sculpture

Tokiwa Fantasia Working Committee (Japan) used 12, 120 two-liter plastic bottles to build a sculpture that stood 37 ft. 3 in. (11.37 m) in Ube, Japan, in 2010.

Photo: Guinness World Records Limited

Did You Know?
The sculpture was named *Tokyo Sky Tree*.

ACTIVITIES

1. Was the number of bottles used for the sculpture closer to 10,000 or 15,000?

_____

2. Write estimates of the number of plastic bottles used in your home.

Each Week: Each Month: Each Year:

Longest Model Train

Photo: Guinness World Records Limited

A model train measuring 892 ft. 3 in. (271.97 m) long was built by Miniature Wunderland GmbH in an arena in Hamburg, Germany, in 2008.

Did You Know?
The train included eight engines and 2,212 cars.

ACTIVITIES

1. About how many cars were pulled by each engine? Round to the nearest whole number.

   _____

2. Some people collect miniature animal figurines, football helmets, or airplanes. Describe a miniature you own.

   _____

3. What is frequently transported by train?

   _____

Largest Painting by Numbers

Photo: Guinness World Records Limited

Ecole de Dessin, a school in Lagos State, Nigeria, unveiled a paint-by-numbers artwork with an area of 33,696 sq. ft. 138.2 sq. in. (3,130.55 m²) on November 17, 2010.

Did You Know?
The painting depicted the map and flag of Nigeria.

ACTIVITIES

1. There are more than 50 countries on the African continent. Look at a map. Write the name of a third nation for each region.

   North Africa: Libya, Algeria, _____

   West Africa: Nigeria, Senegal, _____

   East Africa: Ethiopia, Eritrea, _____

   South Africa: Namibia, Mozambique, _____

2. Write the name of the African country you would most like to visit.

   _____

74

Largest Model of a Human Organ

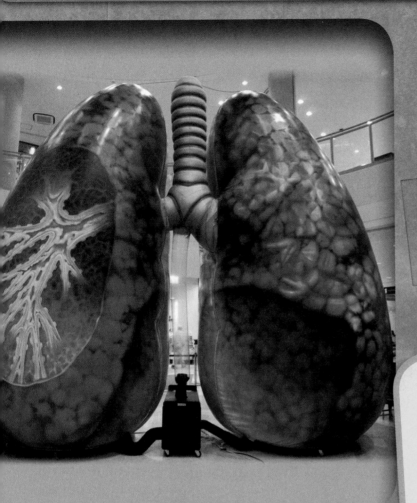

In Sapporo, Hokkaido, Japan, Pfizer Japan Inc. created a model of human lungs that measured 16 ft. 5 in. (5.02 m) tall and 18 ft. 11 in. (5.78 m) wide in 2010.

Did You Know?

The model showed a healthy lung on one side and a smoker's lung on the other.

Photo: Guinness World Records Limited

ACTIVITIES

1. Exercise keeps your lungs healthy. Circle your favorite ways to exercise.

   playing tag   **dancing**

   practicing karate   **playing soccer**

   swimming   **riding a bike**

2. Unscramble the names of human organs.

   ethar _____   **tahmosc** _____

   gunl _____   **denyik** _____

Longest Chain of Bracelets

Photo: AP

The longest chain of bracelets consisted of 3,799 friendship bracelets assembled by 600 students at Owingsville Elementary School (USA) in Owingsville, Kentucky. The participating students from kindergarten through grade 5 were winners of the Carson-Dellosa Classroom Challenge contest.

Did You Know?
Friendship bracelets began in Central and South America. People used to tie on a friendship bracelet and make a wish.

CHECK THIS OUT!

Who is your best friend? The students at Owingsville Elementary School (United States) could be the best of friends! In May 2011, they worked together to create the world's Longest Chain of Bracelets. Students created a total of 3,799 links that were connected to make one long bracelet. The bracelet measured 810 feet long—the entire length of the school's outdoor running track!

The idea for the bracelet came about after the school hosted a Friendship Day. During Friendship Day, students in different grade levels were able to create new friendships. The students wanted to create a symbol to celebrate the day, which led to the world record!

ACTIVITIES

1. If 600 students were in charge of assembling the same number of friendship bracelets, how many was each student in charge of? Round to the nearest hundredth.

   a. 6.3 bracelets

   b. 6.33 bracelets

   c. 3.66 bracelets

   d. 3.7 bracelets

2. Finish the sentence.

   The idea for the bracelet came about after Owingsville

   Elementary School hosted a _____ .

3. Is 810 feet more or less than a quarter-mile? Circle your answer.

   more   less

4. Create a chain using strips of construction paper and glue or tape. Take a strip of paper and glue or tape both ends together so that it forms a circle. Then, take another strip of paper and link it through the circle before gluing its ends together. Continue the chain until you run out of paper. How long is your chain?

   _____

5. What are three adjectives you can use to describe your best friend?

   _____   _____   _____

6. Think of something you could give a friend as a symbol of your friendship. Draw it here.

Fastest Marathon by a Marching Band

Photo: Guinness World Records Limited

Twenty members of the Huddersfield University Marching Band (UK) completed a marathon in 7 hours 55 minutes while playing their instruments in London, United Kingdom, on April 17, 2011.

Did You Know?

The Rose Parade happens in Pasadena, California, every January. Many of the nation's best marching bands are invited each year.

ACTIVITIES

1. How many minutes did it take the band to complete the marathon?

   _____

2. There are about 26 miles in a marathon. About what part of a mile did the band complete each minute?

   _____

3. How many fewer minutes would make the band's marathon time six hours?

   _____

Tallest Sandcastle

Photo: Guinness World Records Limited

Ed Jarrett (USA) created a sandcastle that measured 37 ft. 10 in. (11.53 m) tall in Farmington, Connecticut, in 2011.

Did You Know?

Over 1.5 million pounds of sand and water were used in the construction of the sandcastle.

ACTIVITIES

1. Would you rather build a sandcastle close to the ocean, where the tide will eventually wash it away, or farther back on the beach where it will be protected? Explain your answer.

_____

_____

2. Make a castle or other building from sand, clay, or cardboard. Draw a picture of your creation.

Largest Collection of Model Cars

Photo: Guinness World Records Limited

Nabil Karam (Lebanon) owns a collection of model cars that contains at least 27,777 unique items.

Did You Know?

Karam told the officials to stop counting cars at 27,777.

ACTIVITIES

1. Do you have lots of action figures, blocks, coins, or books? Think of one collection of things at your home. Estimate how many items it contains.

   _____

2. Now, count your collection. How many actual items did you count?

   _____

3. How close was your estimate? Circle your answer.

   within 10   **within 20**   **within 50**

Largest Underwater Painting

Photo: Guinness World Records Limited

Alexander Belazor (Ukraine) created a 8.61-sq.-ft. (0.8-m^2) painting while diving in the Red Sea off the coast of Egypt in 2010.

Did You Know?

Belazor's painting showed a fish swimming in the ocean.

ACTIVITIES

1. What hobby or talent do you think you could carry out while underwater?

   _____

2. Egypt is at the top of what large continent?

   _____

3. What is more remarkable—making a painting that has an area of 8.61 square feet, or making a painting while underwater? Explain your answer.

   _____

Largest Toast Mosaic

The largest toast mosaic measured 1,378.31 sq. ft. (128.05 m²) and was achieved by Laura Hadland (UK) in Warrington, United Kingdom, on October 17, 2010.

Photo: Guinness World Records Limited

Did You Know?

In one year, farmers in Kansas produced enough wheat to make 36.5 billion loaves of bread. That's five loaves of bread for every person on Earth!

CHECK THIS OUT!

Laura Hadland (United Kingdom) set a world record when she created a birthday gift for her mother-in-law. The 27-year-old museum curator turned a photo of her mother-in-law, Sandra Whitfield, into the world's Largest Toast Mosaic. Hadland used 9,852 slices of toast. That was more than 600 loaves of bread!

Hadland, with the help of 40 friends, used nine toasters to brown the slices of bread. They toasted some slices more than others so there were a variety of shades of brown to choose from. After spending six hours working on the mosaic, Hadland surprised her husband's mother with the portrait to celebrate her 50th birthday. That is one unique present!

CRAZY
CREATIONS

ACTIVITIES

1. Think of the best birthday present you've ever given someone. How did that person react? How did it make you feel?

   _____

   _____

2. Use three adjectives to describe the Largest Toast Mosaic.

   _____   _____   _____

3. What would you do if you were able to hang out with 40 of your closest friends?

   _____

   _____

4. Ask an adult to make two pieces of toast. Using only your teeth, bite the toast into different shapes and sizes. What does your toast creation look like? Draw it here.

5. If Hadland used 600 loaves of bread in her toast mosaic, how many slices of bread were there in each loaf? Round to the nearest hundredth.

   a. 16.4 slices

   b. 26.4 slices

   c. 26.42 slices

   d. 16.42 slices

6. Finish the sentence.

   Hadland is _____ years younger than her mother-in-law.

Largest Rocking Horse

Photo: Guinness World Records Limited

On September 12, 2010, Ofer Mor (Israel) finished building a rocking horse that was 24 ft. 11 in. (7.6 m) long and 20 ft. (6.10 m) tall.

Did You Know?
There is evidence that children in ancient Greece and Egypt played with toy horses on wheels.

ACTIVITIES

1. Each floor, or story, of a building is about 10 feet tall. How many stories tall is the Largest Rocking Horse?

   _____

2. Would you rather ride on the Largest Rocking Horse or explore the Largest Cardboard Box Sculpture (page 68)? Explain your answer.

   _____

   _____

   _____

Largest Button Mosaic

Photo: Guinness World Records Limited

Over six days in 2006, a mosaic made from 296,981 buttons was constructed at Maritime Square, Tsing Yi District, Hong Kong, China. The area of the mosaic measured 720 sq. ft. (66.89 m²).

Did You Know?

Thousands of patents related to buttons and clothing fasteners have been issued by the U.S. Patent and Trademark Office.

ACTIVITIES

1. Write <, >, or = to complete the statement.

   296,981 ◯ $\frac{1}{4}$ million

2. Do you have a collection of buttons at your home? Sort buttons (or other items you find) four different times using four different categories. For example, you might sort the items by color, size, or shape. Write the categories you used.

   _____   _____

   _____   _____

Most People Chalk Drawing Simultaneously (Single Location)

Photo: Guinness World Records Limited

On September 20, 2009, 5,391 people drew with chalk on Andrassy Street in Budapest, Hungary, at an event organized by EURÓPA Közhasznú.

Did You Know?
Sidewalk chalk is made from calcium sulfate.

ACTIVITIES

1. Circle what you have drawn, or would like to draw, with sidewalk chalk.

    hopscotch board   **circle for playing marbles**

    hangman or tic-tac-toe   **foursquare board**

    mural or scene   **giant message**

2. If you could have only three colors of sidewalk chalk, what colors would you choose?

———————————   ———————————   ———————————

Largest Collection of Apples

Photo: Guinness World Records Limited

Erika and Kurt Werth (Italy) have been collecting apple-related items for over 30 years. They own 2,300 different artificial apples.

Did You Know?
It takes about 36 apples to produce one gallon of apple cider.

ACTIVITIES

1. How many more artificial apples would the Werths need for a collection of 3,200?

   _____

2. About how many artificial apples did the Werths collect each year? Round to the nearest whole number.

   _____

3. Circle your favorite ways to eat apples.

applesauce	apple slices	apple pie
whole apple	apple butter	apple juice

Largest Handprint Painting

Photo: Guinness World Records Limited

The largest handprint painting is 46,885.98 sq. ft. (4,355.85 m²), and was achieved at an event organized by the Lebanese Red Cross Youth Department, in Beirut, Lebanon, on October 31, 2010.

Did You Know?

The world records for the Biggest Serving of Tabbouleh, the Largest Flag, and the Biggest Bowl of Hummus were all set in Lebanon.

CHECK THIS OUT!

In October 2010, people from all around Lebanon lent a hand to set a Guinness World Record—literally! More than 8,700 people combined their handprints to form the world's Largest Handprint Painting.

The organizers had been planning the event for over a year, but actually creating the handprint painting took only two days. Eight pieces of fabric measuring over 87 yards long and 6 yards wide were sent out to school districts in Lebanon. Thousands of students imprinted their hands on the cloth. Then, the pieces were put together to form the giant painting.

The handprint painting showed the Red Cross symbol surrounded by people from different backgrounds. The message promotes tolerance for people that are different in society.

ACTIVITIES

1. Trace your hand on a piece of paper. Then, trace your friend's hand. Whose hand is bigger?

_____

2. Find eight blank pieces of paper that are all the same size. Draw a picture on each piece, and then combine the sheets of paper into one big drawing. How big is the final work of art?

_____

3. Create your own drawing that promotes tolerance for people that are different in society.

4. In feet and inches, how long were the eight pieces of fabric used in the Largest Handprint Painting?

   a. 261 feet

   b. 261 feet, 3 inches

   c. 18 feet

   d. 18 feet, 6 inches

5. When was the last time you lent a hand to help someone? What did you do and how did it make you feel?

_____

_____

_____

Largest Puppet/Marionette

Photo: Guinness World Records Limited

The mascot for the Ital-Fest in Ottawa, Canada, in 2008, was a marionette that measured 58 ft. 5.5 in. (17 m 82 cm) tall.

Did You Know?
The Ital-Fest celebrates Canadian-Italian heritage. Red, green, and white are the colors of the Italian flag.

ACTIVITIES

1. An oak tree is about 50–60 feet tall. Is the Largest Puppet/Marionette about the same height as an oak tree? Circle your answer.

    yes   **no**

2. Look at a map. What large ocean lies between Europe (where Italy is found) and North America (where Canada is found)?

    _____

3. What states would you need to travel through to reach Canada from your home?

    _____

Largest Confetti Mosaic

Photo: Guinness World Records Limited

In 2008, Nikki Douthwaite (UK) used 587,000 hole-punched dots to create a mosaic 10 ft. 1 in. (3.07 m) wide and 6 ft. 10 in. (2.08 m) tall.

Did You Know?

Douthwaite calls her pieces *dot art*. She created this one as a student at Manchester Metropolitan University.

ACTIVITIES

1. Some people think confetti is fun. Others think it wastes resources and makes a mess. Write your opinion about whether confetti should be used.

   _____

   _____

2. Write four personality traits you think an artist would need to have in order to create a mosaic from confetti.

   _____   _____

   _____   _____

Largest Serving of Meatballs

Photo: Guinness World Records Limited

On May 24, 2009, a serving of meatballs weighing 689 lb. (312.5 kg) was made in Serres, Greece. The meatballs were made with buffalo meat, buffalo milk, parsley, spices, breadcrumbs, and onions.

Did You Know?

In Norway, meatballs are called *meat cakes* and are served with boiled potatoes, gravy, jam, and stewed green peas.

ACTIVITIES

1. If each meatball weighed $\frac{1}{8}$ pound, how many individual meatballs would be in the Largest Serving of Meatballs?

   _____

2. To make meatballs, a meat mixture is usually shaped by hand into round balls. List other foods that are round.

   _____   _____   _____

   _____   _____   _____

Largest Seashell Mosaic

Photo: Guinness World Records Limited

Police officers and others in Dubai, United Arab Emirates, created a seashell mosaic that measured 1,872 sq. ft. (147 m²) in 2009.

Did You Know?
The mosaic contained 59,835 seashells.

ACTIVITIES

Unscramble names of seashells.

conch	sand dollar	cowry	nautilus

ansd roadll _____

woycr _____

honcc _____

situnaul _____

The largest collection of trolls belongs to Sophie Marie Cross (UK). She began collecting in 2003 and, as of December 3, 2009, has 633 unique items.

Photo: Guinness World Records Limited

Did You Know?

It is estimated that 20 million people collect stamps in the United States.

CHECK THIS OUT!

Sophie Marie Cross (United Kingdom) began collecting troll dolls when her brother gave her a small, pencil-topper troll in 2003. She originally set the record for the Largest Collection of Trolls in 2007 with 490, but Cross didn't stop there! Her collection continued to grow and she broke her own record in 2009 with 633 trolls. The most expensive item is a battery-powered troll riding a skateboard.

Cross's collection lives in her bedroom. She owns 57 trolls with orange hair, 81 with yellow hair, 52 with blue hair, 35 with red hair, 39 with green hair, 29 with purple hair, 16 with white hair, 27 with multicolored hair, six with black hair, two with gray hair, and 229 with pink hair!

1. Complete the crossword puzzle with words you read on page 94.

Across

3. Cross's collection lives in this room of her house.

4. Cross's most expensive troll is riding a _____.

6. Where Cross lives

7. What Cross collects

8. Cross has 52 trolls with _____ hair.

Down

1. Cross's first troll in her collection was a _____ troll.

2. Cross's first and middle name

5. The most popular hair color in Cross's collection

2. Number the amount of troll dolls Cross has in each color from least to greatest. Write *1* on the hair color of which Cross has the least, and *11* on the hair color of which she has the most.

_____ orange   _____ green   _____ black

_____ yellow   _____ purple   _____ gray

_____ blue   _____ white   _____ pink

_____ red   _____ multicolored

Largest Horseshoe Sculpture

Photo: Guinness World Records Limited

Donnie Faulk (USA) created a sculpture from 1,071 horseshoes in Pulaski, Tennessee, in 2006.

Did You Know?
Horseshoe crabs were once called *horsefoot crabs* because their shells resemble a horse's hoof.

ACTIVITIES

1. A *hink pink* is a riddle made from rhyming words. Write a word that relates to horses to solve each hink pink clue.

   feet seat _____   **mare chair** _____

   horse course _____   **crude food** _____

2. If 40 horseshoes were used to make each one of the horse's legs, how many horseshoes were used to create the rest of the horse's body?

   _____

Longest Painting by an Individual

Photo: Guinness World Records Limited

In 2008, Tommes Nentwig (Germany) created a painting that measured 6,587 ft. 10 in. (2,008 m) long.

Did You Know?

It took Nentwig one year to complete the entire painting.

ACTIVITIES

1. What three long things could be subjects for three long paintings?

   _____   _____   _____

2. Circle your favorite art materials.

   colored pencils   watercolors   markers

   crayons or pastels   recycled objects   clay

   fabric   acrylic paints   beads

Longest Painting

Photo: Guinness World Records Limited

On May 28, 2010, 3,000 students in San Luis Potosí, Mexico, created a painting that measured 19,689 ft. 11 in. (6,001.5 m) long.

Did You Know?

The painting was done on paper and was all about Mexico, its government, and its people.

ACTIVITIES

1. There are 5,280 feet in a mile. About how many miles long was the Longest Painting? Round to the nearest tenth.

_____

2. Would you rather create a giant artwork by yourself (like Tommes Nentwig, page 97) or with a group? Explain your answer.

_____

_____

_____

Largest Teddy Bear/Soft Toy Mosaic

Photo: Guinness World Records Limited

On July 26, 2008, the
Chelsea Teddy Bear
Company in Michigan
created a teddy bear
mosaic that measured
614 sq. ft. (57.04 m^2).

Did You Know?

The teddy bear got
its name from U.S. President
Theodore Roosevelt.

ACTIVITIES

1. Look at the photo. Circle an estimate of how many teddy bears make
   up the mosaic.

   0-100   **101-300**   **more than 300**

2. Why is it appropriate for a teddy bear mosaic to be in the shape of a
   peace sign? Explain your answer.

   _____

3. Describe your favorite stuffed animal or toy.

   _____

Largest Bean Mosaic

Photo: Guinness World Records Limited

The largest bean mosaic measures 26.25 ft. (8 m) in length, 29.53 ft. (9 m) in width, and was created by C. Vijayalakshmi Prabakaran (India), in Puducherry, India, on December 4, 2010.

Did You Know?
Dried pinto beans are an off-white color and covered with reddish spots. When they are cooked, they turn pink.

CHECK THIS OUT!

Beans come in many shapes and sizes. There are navy beans, kidney beans, black beans, and pinto beans, just to name a few. People often eat them on their own or mixed in with their favorite meal. Beans can be a healthy addition to chili, tacos, or salads. They are a good source of fiber and protein, which your body needs to be strong and healthy.

Beans are very versatile. Besides eating them, C. Vijayalakshmi Prabakaran (India) came up with another use for beans. He used them to create the world's Largest Bean Mosaic. This achievement was created to raise awareness about the "Education For All" campaign. In the mosaic, five different kinds of beans were used to spell the words *1 Goal Education For All.*

1. Why are beans a healthy addition to many popular dishes?

_____

2. Beans are a good source of protein. Name three more foods that are good sources of protein.

_____   _____   _____

3. Circle five words you read on page 100 to complete the word search. Use the word bank to help you.

> kidney   navy   pinto   fiber   protein

X	F	I	B	E	R	W	Z
E	V	X	K	I	I	Y	F
W	P	I	N	T	O	E	P
K	I	D	N	E	Y	L	V
Y	D	N	A	V	Y	Q	D
P	P	R	O	T	E	I	N
J	C	L	P	O	L	H	E
F	R	O	H	S	G	J	G

4. In the mosaic, five different kinds of beans were used to spell the words *1 Goal Education For All*. True or false? Circle your answer.

true   false

5. Design a dinner menu using beans as your main ingredient. What would you serve as your appetizer and main course?

Appetizer: _____

Main Course: _____

6. In square meters, what is the area of the Largest Bean Mosaic?

_____

Largest Orchestra Playing on Recycled Materials

Photo: Guinness World Records Limited

In Kostrzyn, Poland, in 2010, 617 people formed an orchestra known as *Allegro gra Eko* and played recycled materials as instruments.

Did You Know?

The orchestra played an original song, "All for Planet." Many played old computers and printers.

ACTIVITIES

1. Do you reuse plastic grocery bags? Use both sides of printer paper? Use leaves to mulch your plants? Write two ways you and your family recycle to conserve resources.

   _____

   _____

2. The prefix *re-* means "again." Write *re* to complete each word.

   _____store   _____place

   _____fresh   _____search

Largest Awareness Ribbon Made With Flowers

Photo: Guinness World Records Limited

An awareness ribbon made of flowers was created on behalf of the Dubai Healthcare City to raise awareness for breast cancer research. It was unveiled on November 16, 2007. It was 94 ft. 2 in. (28.71 m) long and was made out of 105,000 pink carnations.

Did You Know?

Anna Jarvis founded Mother's Day in 1908 and started the tradition of giving out white carnations to mothers everywhere.

ACTIVITIES

1. Write *0* in each space to complete the number of carnations used in the awareness ribbon.

   1 _____ 5, _____ _____ _____

2. How many years ago was 1908? _____

3. Where do you think the Dubai Healthcare City is located? Explain your answer.

   _____

   _____

Largest Cork Mosaic

Photo: Guinness World Records Limited

In 2008, Saimir Strati (Albania) created a mosaic from 229,675 bottle corks at a hotel in Tirana, Albania.

Did You Know?

Strati also holds the record for the Largest Nail Mosaic.

ACTIVITIES

1. About how many bottle corks did the artist use in each quadrant of the mosaic? Round to the nearest whole number.

   _____

2. With a friend, make a mosaic from squares of colored paper, game pieces, coins, blocks, or other small objects. Explain what you did.

   _____

   _____

Largest Calligraphy Lesson

A calligraphy lesson involving 575 people took place in Kowloon, Hong Kong, China, on December 11, 2010.

Photo: Guinness World Records Limited

Did You Know?
The word *calligraphy* means "beautiful writing." All Chinese children practice calligraphy.

ACTIVITIES

In China, calligraphy is a highly respected art form. A person's writing is said to reveal his or her personality and character. On the lines below, write the quote in your most beautiful handwriting.

Fill your paper with the breathings of your heart.
—William Wordsworth

_____

_____

_____

Largest Button Sculpture

2000

TWENTIETH CENTURY
1900-2000

VICTORIAN
1800-1900

Photo: Guinness World Records Limited

The world's largest 3-D button sculpture was displayed at the People's Museum, Newcastle Upon Tyne, United Kingdom, on January 4, 2000. The exhibition measured approximately 9.8 ft. by 9.8 ft. by 6.5 ft. (3 m by 3 m by 2 m).

Did You Know?

Approximately 1,163,342 buttons were used to create the replica of the sun and planets in our solar system.

CHECK THIS OUT!

If you're going to set the world record for the Largest Button Sculpture, you're going to need a lot of buttons! *Celestial Heavens* used more than one million buttons! Organizers began collecting buttons for the sculpture and added them to those gathered by People's Museum founder Angela Rafferty (United Kingdom). The rest of the buttons were donated by people following ads placed in leaflets, newspapers, and magazines. A washtub was even placed outside the museum for people to leave their buttons!

The buttons were counted, cleaned, sorted, and researched, taking nearly 2,000 hours to complete. In the sculpture, pearl and black buttons are used to represent the night sky. The sun is represented by brass buttons and the planets are covered in buttons of colors of their respective hues.

1. Name the eight planets in the solar system.

_____   _____

_____   _____

_____   _____

_____   _____

2. The world's Largest Button Sculpture took more than one million hours to complete. True or false? Circle your answer.

true   **false**

3. What was not a way organizers collected buttons?

   a. A washtub was placed outside the museum.

   b. Ads were placed in leaflets, newspapers, and magazines.

   c. The museum founder donated buttons she had gathered.

   d. Organizers removed buttons from unwanted clothing.

4. Finish the sentence.

   The world's Largest Button Sculpture is called _____ .

5. Draw wacky buttons on this shirt.

6. About how many days is 2,000 hours? Round to the nearest tenth.

_____

Photo: Guinness World Records Limited

A chain of 2,192 bandanas was formed in Tokyo, Japan, on December 24, 2009. It was 4,855 ft. 7 in. (1,480 m) long.

Did You Know?
Bandanas are popularly used as head wraps and neck scarfs. In a pinch, they can be napkins, washcloths, or arm slings.

ACTIVITIES

1. Give the length of the bandana chain in inches.

   _____

2. About how many inches long was each bandana? Round to the nearest tenth.

   _____

3. Look at a map. Circle the region of Japan where Tokyo is found.

   North   **South**   **East**   **West**

Largest Anamorphic Pavement Art

Photo: Guinness World Records Limited

In the Netherlands in 2009, Planet Streetpainting unveiled a circular anamorphic artwork showing planet Earth. It measured 8,072.9 sq. ft. (750 m²).

Did You Know?
Anamorphic art is 3-D art best viewed from a certain angle.

ACTIVITIES

Find a 3-D object such as a toy car, a stuffed animal, or a piece of fruit. Look at the object carefully from all angles. In the boxes below, draw what you see.

Front or Back View   **Side View**   **Top View**   **Bottom View**

Largest Pencil Mosaic

Photo: Guinness World Records Limited

Students in the country of Kuwait made the largest pencil mosaic in 2010. It measured 467 sq. ft. 83 sq. in. (43.44 m²).

ACTIVITIES

1. About how many pencils did each student contribute to the mosaic? Round to the nearest whole number.

   _____

2. There were 1,025,000 pencils used. Circle the number in the ten thousands place.

   1   **2**   **0**

3. Look at a map. What large Middle Eastern country lies to the south of Kuwait?

   _____

Tallest Indoor Music Fountain

Photo: Guinness World Records Limited

An indoor music fountain with a water column height of up to 59 ft. 8 in. (18.2 m) was installed at a department store in Busan, South Korea, in 2010.

Did You Know?
Music fountains combine water, laser lights, and sounds into dazzling shows.

ACTIVITIES

Choreograph your own musical fountain. Draw lines to connect items in each column. Write your own ideas on the blank lines.

Water Type	Laser Images	Music Type
mist	jumping animals	pop music
falling water	dots and waves	piano music
shooting water	stars and asteroids	electronic music
_____	_____	_____

Largest Shirt Mosaic

ONWARD COULEURS PAR Jean Gabriel Causse

Photo: Guinness World Records Limited

The largest shirt mosaic was made using 2,070 shirts in Chiyoda-ku, Tokyo, Japan, on May 14, 2010.

Did You Know?

There are about 1,500 earthquakes every year in Japan.

CHECK THIS OUT!

What do you think of when you hear the word *shirt*? What image pops into your mind? Is it of a short-sleeved T-shirt or a long-sleeved button-up shirt? Maybe it's of a tank top or a sweatshirt. No matter what the word *shirt* makes you think about, the Largest Shirt Mosaic is probably something totally different!

A Japanese clothing company created the mosaic with polo shirts in 24 different colors. The company used 2,070 polo shirts that were specially dyed for the mosaic. After the record was set, the limited-edition shirts were sold online.

The mosaic was 45 shirts tall and 46 shirts wide—almost a perfect square! Its dimensions were 32 feet, 6 inches by 33 feet, 3 inches.

ACTIVITIES

1. Go through your closet and pull out old T-shirts that you haven't worn in a year or longer. What creative way can you reuse them?

   _____

2. Go to a store that sells clothing and estimate how many shirts they have for sale. Do you estimate that it's more or less than 2,070 shirts? Circle your answer.

   more   **less**

3. Would you have wanted to buy one of the limited-edition shirts? Explain why or why not.

   _____

   _____

4. The shirt mosaic was over 32 feet tall and over 33 feet wide. Was it taller or shorter than a 10-story building? Circle your answer.

   taller   **shorter**

5. If the mosaic used 2,070 shirts in 24 different colors, about how many shirts were used of each color? Round to the nearest hundredth.

   a. 86.3 shirts

   b. 85.25 shirts

   c. 86.25 shirts

   d. 85.3 shirts

6. Design your own one-of-a-kind shirt.

Photo: Guinness World Records Limited

Joshua Mueller of Lakewood, Washington, has 403 different pairs of Converse shoes. He has been collecting them since 1991.

Did You Know?

The famous canvas and rubber shoes made by Converse are sometimes called *Chuck Taylors, All Stars, Chucks,* or *Cons.*

ACTIVITIES

1. If Mueller's shoe collection contained 31 different colors, how many pairs of each color would he have?

   _____

2. If 285 pairs of the shoes were high-tops, how many pairs would be some other style?

   _____

3. Is the state of Washington closer to the Atlantic Ocean or the Pacific Ocean?

   _____

Tallest Bread Sculpture

Photo: Guinness World Records Limited

At the Johnson and Wales University College of Culinary Arts in Providence, Rhode Island, in 2010, Ciril Hitz, Mitch Stamm, and Robert Zielinski (all USA) made an all-bread sculpture that measured 18 ft. 3.75 in. (5.58 m) tall.

Did You Know?

A Scandinavian tradition says that if a boy and a girl eat from the same loaf of bread, they are bound to fall in love.

ACTIVITIES

Bread is eaten all over the world. Match each type of bread with its country of origin. Draw a star beside your favorite kind of bread.

Bread	Country of Origin
naan	Germany
rye	United States
cornbread	Israel
focaccia	Italy
soda bread	India
pita	Ireland

Largest Car Mosaic

Photo: Guinness World Records Limited

Four hundred sixty Volkswagen cars made up a mosaic in São Paulo, Brazil, on April 10, 2010.

Did You Know?

The mosaic displayed the logo of the Volkswagen Gol, a car model that was celebrating its 30th anniversary.

ACTIVITIES

1. If the mosaic contained 18 rows of cars, about how many were in each row? Round to the nearest whole number.

_____

2. If the mosaic contained 24 columns of cars, about how many were in each column? Round to the nearest whole number.

_____

3. Write what you can spell with toy cars, blocks, or other small objects.

_____

Largest Papier Mâché Sculpture

Photo: Guinness World Records Limited

In 2010, students and teachers at Salem Lutheran School in Orange, California, created a papier mâché sculpture 7 ft. 5.5 in. (2.27 m) tall with a circumference of 28 ft. 1 in. (8.55 m).

Did You Know?
The sculpture showed planet Earth.

ACTIVITIES

With adult help, make your own papier mâché planet. Blow up a balloon. Tear strips of newspaper, paper towel, or printer paper. In a disposable container, mix $\frac{1}{2}$ glue and $\frac{1}{2}$ water. Dip strips into the mixture and smooth them in 2–3 overlapping layers to cover the balloon. Allow to dry for 1–2 days, then pop the balloon. Use paint or markers to decorate your planet. Draw your creation here.

Largest Matchstick Model

Photo: Guinness World Records Limited

The largest matchstick model consists of 4.075 million matchsticks. It was made by David Reynolds (UK) and was completed in July 2009.

Did You Know?
The model depicts a North Sea oil production platform, where Reynolds used to work.

CHECK THIS OUT!

David Reynolds's (United Kingdom) world record for the Largest Matchstick Model was 15 years in the making.

Reynolds worked on the model, named *Cathedrals of the Sea*, between 2 and 10 hours a day for 15 years. He estimates that he spent 32,000 hours on the project, as well as more than $7,000 on glue and matchsticks!

While working on the model, it became so big that Reynolds had to split it up into 14 sections to store throughout his house! Today, the model is in one piece and is on public display at a museum in the United Kingdom. The model weighs more than one ton and is 12 feet tall and 21 feet long.

1. Create a model with craft sticks and glue or tape. Give your model a name. Draw it here.

2. How many days are there in 32,000 hours? Round to the nearest hundredth.

_____

3. If Reynolds spent $7,000 on his project over the course of 15 years, how much money did he spend per year? Circle your answer.

more than $500   **less than $500**

4. Unscramble words you read on page 118.

takscmhtsic _____   **ulge** _____

esummu _____   **edoml** _____

5. The Largest Matchstick Model is on display in 14 different sections of a museum. True or false? Circle your answer.

true   **false**

6. Imagine your life 15 years from now. How old will you be? What do you think you will be doing? What are some goals you want to accomplish between now and then?

_____

_____

_____

A ② STABILO NEKED IS ÖRÖMTELI VAKÁCIÓT KÍVÁN

Készült a ◆ STABILO
megbízásából 2009. június 24-27-ig
a gyarmati Kossuth Lajos Általános Iskolában.

Photo: Guinness World Records Limited

In 2009, 90 children from two schools in Gyarmat, Hungary, used 300,000 sequins to create a mosaic 6 ft. 6 in. (2 m) tall and 9 ft. 10 in. (3 m) long.

Did You Know?
The mosaic wished all the children a happy summer holiday.

ACTIVITIES

1. *Sequins* are tiny discs of sparkly metal or plastic. They are often used to decorate fabric. Write what you would like to decorate with sequins.

   _____

2. Give the length and height of the mosaic in inches.

   _____

3. Now, give the area of the mosaic in square inches.

   _____

Largest Wooden Sculpture

Photo: Guinness World Records Limited

In 2008, Michel Schmid (Switzerland) created a wooden sculpture of a Sioux Indian head measuring 75 ft. 2 in. (22.92 m).

Did You Know?

The Sioux people lived in the area that is now Wisconsin, Minnesota, North Dakota, and South Dakota.

ACTIVITIES

1. Give the height of the sculpture in inches.

   _____

2. The average adult male in the U.S. is 69 inches tall. About how many average adult men would it take to equal the height of the statue? Round to the nearest whole number.

   _____

3. Write three things that are made from wood.

   _____   _____   _____

Largest Ceramic Mosaic

Photo: Guinness World Records Limited

In 2010, Vietnamese artist Nguyen Thu Thuy directed the creation of a ceramic mosaic on the walls of the Red River Dike in Hanoi, Vietnam, that measured 16,901 sq. ft. 70.86 sq. in. (1,570.2 m²).

Did You Know?
The mural covered up illegal graffiti and advertising along the Red River Dike.

ACTIVITIES

The mosaic in Hanoi celebrates the culture of Vietnam by depicting a local river and other geographical features, animals, and customs. Think about the neighborhood or city where you live. What pictures would best represent its culture? Write your ideas.

1. _____

2. _____

3. _____

4. _____

Longest Drawing

Photo: Guinness World Records Limited

In Coimbatore, India, in 2009, 7,200 people worked together to create a drawing 30,032 ft. 9 in. (9,154 m) long.

Did You Know?

It took four hours and three minutes to complete the drawing, which was titled *Gateway 2009*.

ACTIVITIES

1. How many more people would have made the total number of artists 10,000?

   _____

2. The Longest Drawing was about 30,032 feet. How many feet of drawing did each person complete?

   _____

3. A standard sheet of paper is 11 inches long. How many sheets would you have to tape together to make $5\frac{1}{2}$ feet?

   _____

Largest Pushpin Mosaic

Photo: Guinness World Records Limited

Over 10 months in 2008-2009, 210 members of the Junior Chamber International JB Entrepreneur in Malaysia used pushpins to create a mosaic 30 ft. 8 in. (9.35 m) by 21 ft. 11 in. (6.7 m).

Did You Know?
The mosaic was made up of 3.7 million pushpins.

ACTIVITIES

Unscramble names of school and office supplies.

nelcip _____

huspnip _____

lurer _____

palestr _____

luge _____

rasemkr _____

Photo: Guinness World Records Limited

STUNNING DISTANCES

Photo: Guinness World Records Limited

Longest Swim Under Ice
(Breath Held)

Photo: Guinness World Records Limited

Stig Åvall Severinsen (Denmark) swam 236 ft. 22 in. (72 m) under ice in Knudssø, Ry, Denmark, on March 6, 2010.

Did You Know?
The under-ice swim lasted for 86 seconds.

ACTIVITIES

1. Would you rather swim in water that is warm or cool? Explain your answer.

   _____

2. If a swimming pool lap is 25 meters long, how many laps did Severinsen complete while swimming under ice?

   _____

3. Look at a map. Based on Denmark's location, do you think ice is commonly found there? Circle your answer.

yes   no

Highest Altitude Reached by Helium-Filled Party Balloons

Photo: Guinness World Records Limited

In 2001, Mike Howard (UK) and Steve Davis (USA) ascended to a height of 18,300 ft. (5,777.85 m) using helium-filled latex toy balloons near Albuquerque, New Mexico.

Did You Know?

One thousand four hundred balloons were used for the attempt.

ACTIVITIES

Different types of clouds form at each level of the atmosphere. Draw a balloon next to the clouds to show how high Howard and Davis ascended using balloons.

High Clouds: Cirrus
Above 18,000 feet

Middle Clouds: Alto
6,500–18,000 feet

Low Clouds: Stratus
Up to 6,500 feet

Photo: Guinness World Records Limited

Alfred Sleep (USA) jumped a garbage truck a distance of 77 ft. 4 in. (23.57 m) at Lebanon Valley Speedway in New York in 2004.

Did You Know?
The garbage truck landed on top of a parked car.

ACTIVITIES

1. If an average car is 15 feet long, about how many car lengths did the garbage truck jump?

_____

2. In a ramp jump, a vehicle accelerates up the ramp, sails through the air, and then crashes down on the other side. Which part do you think would be the most fun? Explain your answer.

_____

_____

Greatest Distance on a Snowmobile in 24 Hours

Photo: Guinness World Records Limited

In 2011, Nicholas Musters (Canada) traveled 1,907.06 mi. (3,069.12 km) in 24 hours on a snowmobile in Lake of Bays, Ontario, Canada.

Did You Know?

Musters completed 303 laps on a 6.29-mi. (10.129-km) course.

ACTIVITIES

1. How many laps did Musters complete each hour?

_____

2. How many miles did Musters travel each hour?

_____

3. Circle a vehicle you would like to ride on for 24 hours.

helicopter   racecar   Jet Ski

submarine   garbage truck   hot air balloon

129

Farthest Distance Climbed on a Ladder in Eight Hours (Team)

Photo: Guinness World Records Limited

The farthest distance climbed on a ladder in eight hours by a team of 10 was 25.83 mi. (41.57 km). The record was achieved by members of Kent Fire & Rescue Service (UK) in Ashford, United Kingdom, on August 28, 2010.

Did You Know?

In 2008, more than 25 million calls were made to fire departments. Of those calls, only about 1.5 million were actual fires. Nine percent of the calls were false alarms.

CHECK THIS OUT!

Firefighters are very important people in society. They help put out fires and rescue people from burning buildings. They also teach about fire safety so people know how to prevent fires and know what to do if a fire were to happen.

In August 2010, a team of 10 firefighters made their way into the record books by setting the world record for Farthest Distance Climbed on a Ladder in Eight Hours. The team members from Kent Fire & Rescue Service (United Kingdom) climbed almost 26 miles! The attempt was made after fire service teams in Sydney, Australia, and New York City said that they would like to begin an international competition over this record with the team from Kent.

ACTIVITIES

1. Do some research on fire safety. What are two ways to prevent fires around your home?

   1. _____

   2. _____

2. When was the last time you were in a competition with another person or group? Describe it. Did competing with another person push you to perform at your very best?

   _____

   _____

   _____

3. How many feet are in 26 miles?

   a. 173,820 feet

   b. 137,280 feet

   c. 173,280 feet

   d. 137,820 feet

4. What do you want to be when you grow up? Do you think you would like to be a firefighter? Explain why or why not.

   _____

   _____

   _____

5. If nine percent of the 25 million calls to fire departments were false alarms, how many calls were false alarms?

   _____

6. Three kinds of fire trucks are pumper trucks, ladder trucks, and tanker trucks. Tanker trucks can hold 1,000 gallons of water. If a tanker truck is one-third full, how much water does it carry?

   _____

Longest Nonstop Ocean Voyage by a Raft

Photo: Guinness World Records Limited

In 2002-2003, the raft *Nord*, captained by Andrew Urbanczyk (USA), sailed for 136 days from Half Moon Bay, California, to the Pacific island of Guam.

Did You Know?

The raft, made from seven sequoia redwood logs, measured 39 ft. by 49 ft. (11.9 m by 14.9 m). It traveled 7,767 mi. (12,499 km).

ACTIVITIES

1. Give the area of the *Nord* in square feet.

   _____

2. Look at a world map or globe. With your finger, trace the route of the *Nord*. What island in the Pacific Ocean would you like to visit?

   _____

3. Build a raft from twigs, string, and a piece of foam. Does your raft float? Circle your answer.

   yes   no

Fastest Conventional Motorcycle Speed (Female)

Photo: Guinness World Records Limited

Leslie Porterfield (USA) piloted a motorcycle that traveled 232.522 mph (374.208 km/h) at Bonneville Salt Flats, Utah, on September 5, 2008.

Did You Know?
Porterfield drove a modified Suzuki Hayabusa.

ACTIVITIES

1. How many miles per hour are vehicles allowed to travel on a highway near your home?

   _____

2. Use your answer to #1. How many miles per hour faster did Porterfield's motorcycle travel?

   _____

3. Do you think roads should have speed limits? Explain your answer.

   _____

Fastest Vehicle Crossing of the Great Sand Sea (Sahara)

Photo: Guinness World Records Limited

In 2009, Hesham Nessim (Egypt) traveled between the Gilf Kebir Plateau and the Siwa Oasis in Egypt in 5 hours 33 minutes.

Did You Know?

The Great Sand Sea is part of the Sahara Desert. The size of New Mexico, it is the third largest accumulation of sand in the world.

ACTIVITIES

1. Write a list of things you would pack for a trip across the Great Sand Sea.

   _____ _____ _____

   _____ _____ _____

2. How is the Great Sand Sea like an ocean?

   _____

3. On what continent can you find the Sahara Desert?

   _____

Fastest Crossing of Canada on Foot (Female)

Photo: Guinness World Records Limited

Over 143 days in 2002, Anne Keane (Canada) ran across Canada from St. John's, Newfoundland, to Tofino, British Columbia. She ran for 4,866 mi. (7,831 km).

Did You Know?
Keane ran for all but three of the 143 days.

ACTIVITIES

1. Circle the side of Canada on which Keane began her journey.

   east   **west**

2. Circle the side of Canada on which Keane ended her journey.

   east   **west**

3. What ocean did Keane see at the beginning of her journey? What ocean did she see at the end?

   _____

Greatest Distance Traveled on a Treadmill in 24 Hours (Female)

Photo: Guinness World Records Limited

The greatest distance traveled on a treadmill in 24 hours by a woman is 153.6 mi. (247.2 km) by Edit Berces (Hungary) in Budapest, Hungary, on March 8–9, 2004.

Did You Know?

An *ultramarathon* is any sporting event involving running longer than the traditional marathon length of 26.2 miles.

CHECK THIS OUT!

Edit Berces is an ultramarathon runner from Hungary. In March 2004, Berces set the record for the Greatest Distance Traveled on a Treadmill in 24 Hours for a Female. At the time, this record was the overall record for an individual. However, that record was broken by Arulanantham Suresh Joachim (Australia) in November 2004, when he ran a distance of 160.24 miles.

During Berces's 24-hour attempt, she also broke the record for the Fastest Time to Run 100 Kilometers on a Treadmill and the Fastest Time to Run 100 Miles on a Treadmill for a Female. She reached the 100-kilometer mark at 8 hours, 35 minutes, 5 seconds and the 100-mile mark at 14 hours, 15 minutes, 8 seconds.

ACTIVITIES

1. There are 0.62 miles in one kilometer. How many miles are there in 100 kilometers? Circle your answer.

more than 60 miles　　　　　**less than 60 miles**

2. How many more miles did Joachim run in 24 hours than Berces?

a. 6.64 miles

b. 4.66 miles

c. 60.24 miles

d. 134.04 miles

3. Look at a map of your state. What city is about 150 miles away from where you live?

_____

4. Fill in vowel letters to complete words you read on page 136.

☐ltr☐m☐r☐th☐n　　r☐nn☐r

5. Circle the months that Berces held the record for Greatest Distance Traveled on a Treadmill in 24 Hours by an Individual.

January	May	September
February	June	October
March	July	November
April	August	December

6. Would you want to be an ultramarathon runner? Explain why or why not.

_____

_____

Farthest Distance
Side-Wheel Driving (Truck)

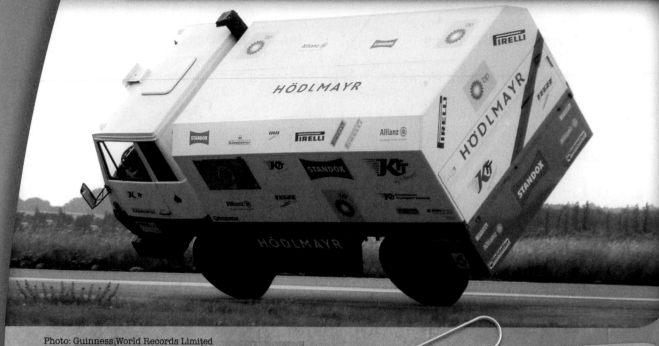

Photo: Guinness World Records Limited

On June 18, 2004, Johann Redl (Austria) drove a delivery truck a distance of 10.19 mi. (16.4 km) on two wheels.

Did You Know?
The delivery truck weighed 16,358 lb. (7,420 kg).

ACTIVITIES

1. Play with a toy vehicle. Write a good tip or strategy for getting it to roll on two wheels.

   _____

2. Which is more likely to fall: a two-wheeled vehicle or a four-wheeled vehicle? Explain your answer.

   _____

   _____

   _____

Greatest Distance Cartwheeling in 24 Hours (Team)

Photo: Guinness World Records Limited

In 2006, a team of 10 people from Beausejour Gymnos (Canada) traveled 31 mi. (50 km) by doing cartwheels for 24 hours.

Did You Know?

The cartwheeling team included both males and females.

ACTIVITIES

1. Measure the length of a room or an area outside. Can you cartwheel somersault across this distance? Write how far you traveled.

_____

2. Try all these tricks. Circle the one you can perform the best

handstand	crab walk
standing on one foot	cartwhe
somersault	walking backwar
push-up	skipping

Longest Journey in an Excavator/Digger

Photo: Guinness World Records Limited

Between March 26 and April 20, 2010, Neil Smith (USA) drove an excavator from Tybee Island, Georgia, to Ontario, California, a distance of 3,185.9 mi. (5,127.22 km).

Did You Know?
Smith made his journey to raise money for earthquake victims in Haiti.

ACTIVITIES

1. For about how many days did Smith travel in his excavator?

   _____

2. Look at a map of the United States. What states did Smith probably travel through on his journey from Georgia to California?

   _____   _____   _____

   _____   _____   _____

Longest Distance Walking Over Hot Plates

The longest distance walking over hot plates is 75 ft. 1 in. (22.90 m) and was achieved by Rolf Iven (Germany) in Milan, Italy, on April 18, 2009.

Photo: Guinness World Records Limited

Did You Know?
The hot plates had temperatures ranging from 266°–302°F (130°–150°C).

ACTIVITIES

1. Water boils at 212°F. Could you boil water on the hot plates that Iven walked across?

   yes   no

2. Do you think Iven tried to walk across the hot plates slowly or quickly? Explain your answer.

   _____

   _____

   _____

Longest Ocean Swim

Photo: Guinness World Records Limited

The longest distance ever swum without flippers in open sea is 139.8 mi. (225 km) by Veljko Rogosic (Croatia) across the Adriatic Sea from August 29–31, 2006.

Did You Know?

It is estimated that 65,000 people in the United States do not know how to swim.

CHECK THIS OUT!

Veljko Rogosic (Croatia) holds the world record for the Longest Ocean Swim. In August 2006, he swam from Grado, Italy, to Riccione, Italy, a distance of nearly 140 miles. The attempt took him 50 hours, 10 minutes. That's more than two whole days!

Rogosic isn't the only one to set a world record in the Adriatic Sea. The Greatest Distance Wakeboarding in 24 Hours by a Male was set by Igor Deranja (Croatia) in the Adriatic Sea on September 15–16, 2010. He traveled 319.38 miles during his world record attempt. Deranja was towed on a wakeboard between the cities of Crikvenica, Croatia, and Pula, Croatia. He also wakeboarded around an open water circuit in the city of Poreč, Croatia, midway through the journey.

ACTIVITIES

1. Find the Adriatic Sea on a map. Name two countries it borders.

   1. _____

   2. _____

2. If Rogosic swam 140 miles in 50 hours, what was his average speed in miles per hour? Round to the nearest tenth.

   a. 36 mph

   b. 0.4 mph

   c. 2.8 mph

   d. 3 mph

3. Circle five words you read on page 142 to complete the word search. Use the word bank to help you.

ocean swim Italy Croatia wakeboard

C	R	O	A	T	I	A	X	W
M	V	O	A	E	P	C	O	A
W	W	E	K	M	G	X	E	K
O	I	D	O	W	A	O	S	E
O	P	I	V	G	W	C	W	B
U	E	T	Y	Z	E	E	I	O
K	R	A	H	U	W	A	M	A
J	H	L	Y	W	E	N	C	R
F	T	Y	M	P	T	A	Q	D

4. Do you know how to swim? How long can you swim without stopping or touching the ground? Ask an adult to time you.

   _____

Most Vertical Feet Uphill in Snowshoes in 24 Hours (Female)

Photo: Guinness World Records Limited

In 2009, Eileen Wysocki (USA) wore snowshoes while climbing uphill 25,534 ft. (7,782.8 m) at the Sunlight Mountain Resort in Glenwood Springs, Colorado.

Did You Know?
Early hunters may have invented snowshoes to mimic the ability of animals, like the snowshoe hare, that travel easily in snow.

ACTIVITIES

1. Snowshoes spread out, or *distribute*, your weight so you don't sink into the soft snow. To see how they work, try this experiment with adult permission. In your stocking feet, stand on a short pile of pillows. Have a friend measure. How many inches did you sink down into the pillows?

   _____

2. Now, place something wide, flat, and sturdy (like a carpet square, foam piece, or board) over the pillows and stand on it. How far down did you sink this time?

   _____

Greatest Distance Covered in 24 Hours by Wheelchair

Photo: Guinness World Records Limited

In 2007, Mario Trindade (Portugal) covered a distance of 113.34 mi. (182.4 km) using a wheelchair at a stadium in Vila Real, Portugal.

Did You Know?

In 2011, 32 people who use wheelchairs completed the Boston Marathon.

ACTIVITIES

1. Write the name of a place that is about 115 miles away from your home. If you need help, use a map or ask an adult.

_____

2. Go to www.specialolympics.org and learn about Special Olympics events. Write the names of two sports played by Special Olympics athletes.

_____

_____

Longest Distance Swam Underwater With One Breath (Open Water)

Photo: Guinness World Records Limited

Taking only one breath, Carlos Coste (Venezuela) swam underwater 492 ft. 1 in. (150 m) in the Dos Ojos cave system in Quintana Roo, Mexico, on November 3, 2010.

Did You Know?
Coste's swim lasted 2 minutes 32 seconds.

ACTIVITIES

Deep breathing can help you relax. Deep breaths from the abdomen provide more oxygen than shallow breaths from the chest.

Put your hand on your stomach and inhale deeply through your nose. You should feel your stomach rise. Exhale through your mouth and feel your stomach fall.

Repeat three times. How did the deep breathing make you feel?

_____

_____

Most Vertical Distance Down a Fireman's Pole in One Hour by a Team of 10

Photo: Guinness World Records Limited

A team of 10 firefighters (UK) slid down a fireman's pole a total of 17,191 ft. (5,240 m) in one hour in Hove, United Kingdom, on August 23, 2009.

Did You Know?

Many firefighters have a college degree in fire science.

ACTIVITIES

1. There are 5,280 feet in a mile. How many miles did the team of firefighters slide?

   _____

2. Some firefighters get injured sliding down poles. Many new stations have stairs or slides instead of poles. What do you think is the fastest way to go down: stairs, a slide, or a pole? Explain your answer.

   _____

   _____

Greatest Distance on a Motorcycle in 24 Hours (Individual)

Photo: Guinness World Records Limited

The longest distance driving on a motorcycle in 24 hours is 1,321.65 mi. (2,127 km) and was achieved by Omar Hilal Al-Mamari (Oman) in Oman on August 18–19, 2009.

Did You Know?

Al-Mamari was one of the first people from Oman to set a Guinness World Record.

CHECK THIS OUT!

Omar Hilal Al-Mamari (Oman) earned his spot in the record books by driving the Greatest Distance on a Motorcycle in 24 Hours by an Individual. He drove continuously for more than 1,300 miles between Marmool, Oman, and Thamrait, Oman.

The distance between the two towns is exactly 91.96 miles. The road was an old road that ran parallel to the modern road connecting the two towns. It was sealed off by police for the attempt to avoid putting anyone's safety in danger.

Oman is a country in Southwest Asia, on the coast of the Arabian Peninsula. It borders the United Arab Emirates in the northwest, Saudi Arabia in the west, and Yemen in the southwest.

ACTIVITIES

1. Why was the road sealed off for Al-Mamari's world record attempt? Do you think that was a good idea? Explain why or why not.

_____

_____

_____

2. What does it mean if two roads are *parallel*?

   a. The roads extend in the same direction, but never run into each other.

   b. The roads intersect at 90 degree angles.

   c. The roads cross over each other at least four times.

   d. One road circles the other.

3. How many miles did Al-Mamari travel per hour? Round to the nearest hundredth.

_____

4. Name three countries Oman borders.

   1. _____

   2. _____

   3. _____

5. Name a place you have traveled that is about 92 miles away from home. Ask an adult if you need help.

_____

6. How do you think Al-Mamari reacted after being one of the first people from Oman to set a Guinness World Record? Use three adjectives to describe how he might have felt.

_____   _____   _____

Greatest Distance Moonwalked in One Hour

Photo: Guinness World Records Limited

In 2009, Krunoslav Budiselić (Croatia) moonwalked 3.54 mi. (5.7 km) in one hour at Mladost Stadium in Zagreb, Croatia.

Did You Know?
Pop star Michael Jackson first moonwalked on TV during the 1983 program *Motown 25: Yesterday, Today, Forever.*

ACTIVITIES

1. *Moonwalk* is a compound word formed from two smaller words. Combine these words with *walk* to write more compound words: *side, cross, jay, board, cat, way.*

   _____   _____

   _____   _____

   _____   _____

2. Write a definition for one of the words you wrote above.

   _____

Fastest Circumnavigation by Helicopter

Photo: Guinness World Records Limited

For 17 days 6 hours 14 minutes 25 seconds in 1996, John Williams and Ron Bower (both USA) flew around the world in a westerly direction in a Bell 430 helicopter.

Did You Know?
The journey started and finished in Fair Oaks, London, United Kingdom.

ACTIVITIES

1. Did the helicopter circumnavigation take more than a month or less than a month? Circle your answer.

   more than a month   **less than a month**

2. Would you rather travel around the world in 17 days or 170 days? Explain your answer.

   _____

   _____

   _____

Farthest Distance Static Cycling in 24 Hours by a Team (Male)

Photo: Guinness World Records Limited

Six men on the New York Sports Clubs/Cadence Cycling Team rode static cycles a distance of 829.84 mi. (1,335.5 km) in 24 hours on January 19, 2008.

Did You Know?

You often find static cycles at the gym. They are also called *exercise bikes, stationary bikes, exercycles,* or *spinning machines.*

ACTIVITIES

1. About how many miles did each man on the team ride? Round to the nearest tenth of a mile.

   _____

2. About how many miles did the team ride each hour? Round to the nearest tenth of a mile.

   _____

3. Would you rather ride one mile today inside on a static cycle or outside on a bicycle? Explain your answer.

   _____

Longest Marathon on a Fairground/ Theme Park Attraction

Photo: Guinness World Records Limited

The longest marathon on a traditional fairground attraction lasted 24 hours 30 minutes and was achieved by Brenda Donohue (Ireland) at The Point Village, Dublin, Ireland, on October 23, 2011.

Did You Know?
Donohue rode on a Ferris wheel.

ACTIVITIES

1. The first Ferris wheel was erected in Chicago in 1893. The giant wheel had 36 huge gondolas that could each seat 40 riders. How many people could ride the wheel at once?

   _____

2. Engineer George Ferris invented the Ferris wheel during the late 19th century. Circle the names of other marvels invented around this same time.

   personal computers   **trains**   **electric lights**

   smart phones   **space shuttles**   **telephones**

Fastest Cycle Across the United States

Photo: Guinness World Records Limited

The fastest cycle across the United States from north to south and west to east was achieved by Paul Spencer (UK) in 44 days 1 minute 26 seconds from July 8 through August 21, 2010.

Did You Know?

During this world record attempt, money was raised and donated to three charities: the Lupus Foundation of America, the Boys & Girls Clubs of America, and Disability Snowsport UK.

CHECK THIS OUT!

Paul Spencer (United Kingdom) has been interested in outdoor life since he was a young boy. At nine years old, he learned to play golf and joined the Boy Scouts, which introduced him to climbing, hiking, kayaking, mountain biking, camping, and rugby.

With that in mind, it comes as no surprise that Spencer would set a world record involving the outdoors. He spent more than 44 days cycling across the United States from north to south and west to east. He began his journey in Blaine, Washington, on July 8 and ended in New York City on August 21. Over the course of the 44 days, Spencer traveled a total of 4,662.48 miles through 15 states, and covered an average of 105.96 miles per day!

ACTIVITIES

1. Look at this map of the United States. Color the 15 states Spencer may have ridden through during his world record journey.

2. List states you have visited.

_____   _____   _____

_____   _____   _____

_____   _____   _____

3. Look at a calendar. What date is 44 days from now? What do you think you might be doing that day?

_____

_____

4. Spencer began cycling in Seattle, Washington. True or false? Circle your answer.

true   **false**

5. Fill in vowel letters to complete words you read on page 154.

6. How many more miles would Spencer have needed to ride to reach a total of 4,665 miles?

_____

Longest Motorcycle Ride Through a Tunnel of Fire

Photo: Guinness World Records Limited

On March 13, 2011, Shabir Ahluwalia (India) rode a motorcycle 224 ft. 8 in. (68.49 m) through a tunnel of fire.

Did You Know?

Fire is a chemical reaction between oxygen in the air and a fuel (such as wood or gasoline) that is ignited.

ACTIVITIES

A fire's colors are determined by its fuel source and temperature. Wood contains sodium, which produces yellow and orange flames. Purple and blue flames are the hottest. They can be found near the bottom of a fire, closest to the fuel source. Use the information you read to color the campfire.

Longest Wakeboarding Marathon

Photo: Guinness World Records Limited

Ian Taylor (UK) wakeboarded behind a cable tow for 6 hours 17 minutes on Willen Lake in Buckinghamshire, United Kingdom, in 2004.

Did You Know?
Wakeboarding is a combination of water skiing, snowboarding, and surfing. The rider stands on a wakeboard towed behind a motorboat.

ACTIVITIES

1. Six hours is what fraction of a day?

   _____

2. How many more minutes of wakeboarding would make the record seven hours?

   _____

3. What activity have you spent six hours doing in the past week?

   _____

Farthest Distance Nordic Walking in 24 Hours

Photo: Guinness World Records Limited

Walter Geckle (Austria) used Nordic walking to travel a distance of 108.74 mi. (175 km) in 24 hours in Unzmarkt, Austria, in 2010.

Did You Know?
In Nordic walking, a walker uses poles similar to ski poles. The sport is also called *ski walking*. It provides a full-body workout.

ACTIVITIES

1. Nordic walking can be enjoyed year-round. What is your favorite sport or exercise to do in any season?

_____

2. How many miles did Geckle walk each hour? Round to the nearest tenth of a mile.

_____

3. Name another sport that requires you to hold some type of pole or stick.

_____

Fastest 10 Meters Traveled Carrying a Table and Weight in the Mouth

Photo: Guinness World Records Limited

The fastest 10 m traveled while using the mouth to carry a table with weight on it is 6.57 seconds. It was achieved by Georges Christen (Luxembourg) in Beijing, China, in 2009.

Did You Know?

Masseters, between the cheekbone and jawbone, lift the lower jaw to close the teeth. They are among the strongest muscles in the human body.

ACTIVITIES

1. Is 6.5 seconds a short time or a long time to read a book? Circle your answer.

    short   **long**

2. Is 6.5 seconds a short time or a long time to carry something very heavy? Circle your answer.

    short   **long**

3. Explain your answers to #1 and #2.

_____

Greatest Distance on Inline Skates in One Hour

Photo: Guinness World Records Limited

Mauro Guenci (Italy) covered 24.004 mi. (38.632 km) on inline skates in one hour in Senigallia, Ancona, Italy, on June 11, 2005.

Did You Know?

Studies have shown that one of the safest sports for children of all ages is indoor roller skating.

CHECK THIS OUT!

Zoom! Do you like to roller skate? Mauro Guenci (Italy) does! He set the world record for the Greatest Distance on Inline Skates in One Hour. He completed 36 laps on a 0.78-mile track, traveling a total of 24.004 miles to claim the record.

Guenci, a firefighter, also holds the world record for the Greatest Distance on Inline Skates in 24 Hours. For that record, he traveled 337.773 miles in one day in June 2004.

Inline skates are a type of roller skate. They often have two, three, four, or five wheels arranged in a single line on the bottom of the skate. This design lets you go faster than a traditional roller skate, which has two wheels at the front of the skate and two wheels at the back.

ACTIVITIES

1. Complete the crossword puzzle with words you read on page 160.

Across

2. Guenci traveled 24.004 of these in one hour.

5. Guenci's first name

6. Inline skates are _____ than traditional skates.

7. _____ have two to five wheels in a single line.

8. Guenci set his world record on a _____ .

Down

1. Inline skates are a type of _____ .

3. Guenci is from _____ .

4. Guenci's profession

2. What was Guenci's average speed in miles per hour?

_____ **mph**

3. Do you like to roller skate? Explain why or why not.

_____

_____

Three French women (Stephanie Geyer-Barneix, Alexandra Lux, and Flora Manciet) used their hands to paddleboard 3,001 mi. (4,830 km) from Cape Breton, Canada, to Capbreton, France, in 2009.

Photo: Guinness World Records Limited

Did You Know?
The paddleboard journey took 54 days.

ACTIVITIES

1. Did the paddleboard trip take closer to one month or closer to two months? Circle your answer.

   one month   **two months**

2. The women paddled from the east coast of Canada to the west coast of France. Which ocean did they cross?

   _____

3. Would you rather paddleboard alone or as a member of a team?

   _____

Longest Journey on a Motorized Bicycle

Photo: Guinness World Records Limited

The longest journey on a motorized bicycle was achieved by Eddie Sedgemore (UK), who cycled 1,912.1 mi. (3,077 km) during 28 days in 2009.

Did You Know?

A motorized bicycle is a bicycle with a motor attached. The motor can either power the bike entirely or assist with pedaling.

ACTIVITIES

1. Sedgemore cycled about 1,912 miles in 28 days. How many miles did he travel each day?

   _____

2. Which provides more exercise: riding a standard bicycle or riding a motorized bicycle? Explain your answer.

   _____

   _____

Fastest 100 Meters on a Space Hopper (Male)

Photo: Guinness World Records Limited

Ashrita Furman (USA) used a space hopper to travel 100 m in 30.2 seconds at Flushing Meadow Park, New York, in 2004.

Did You Know?

Other names for the toy called a *space hopper* include *hoppity ball, moon hopper, skippyball,* and *hoppity hop.*

ACTIVITIES

1. There are 3.3 feet in a meter. How many feet did Furman travel on the space hopper?

   _____

2. A yard is three feet. A football field is 100 yards. How many feet make the length of a football field?

   _____

3. Write <, >, or = to complete the statement.

   length of Furman's ride $\bigcirc$ length of a football field

Farthest Distance Static Cycling in 24 Hours by a Team (Female)

Photo: Guinness World Records Limited

Six women on Team CanCare (South Africa) static cycled 722.03 mi. (1,162 km) in 24 hours on November 4-5, 2010, in Honeydew, South Africa.

Did You Know?
A *recumbent* cycle allows the rider to lean back in a lying position.

ACTIVITIES

1. Who achieved a world record first—the women's static cycling team or the men's static cycling team (page 152)?

   _____

2. How many more miles did the men's team ride than the women's team?

   _____

3. How many official languages are spoken in South Africa? Do some research to find out.

   _____

Longest Solo Motorcycle Journey (Female)

Photo: Guinness World Records Limited

Benka Pulko (Slovenia) traveled 111,856 mi. (180,016 km) on her solo motorcycle journey through seven continents. She began her journey in Ptuj, Slovenia, on June 19, 1997, and ended at the same location on December 10, 2002.

Did You Know?

Pulko, who works as a journalist and photographer, took over 35,000 pictures on her journey.

CHECK THIS OUT!

In January 1997, Benka Pulko (Slovenia) decided to ride a motorcycle around the world. At the time, she didn't even know how to ride one! But only five months later, she began her journey that took her through 75 countries and ended with a spot in the record books.

Pulko's trip is believed to be the first ever motorcycle journey to include all seven continents. The trip lasted exactly 2,000 days, or about five-and-a-half years. During that time, Pulko traveled 111,856 miles, averaging 68.35 miles per day over the entire trip. She often spent nights sleeping in her tent or in roadside motels. Between gasoline, photographic equipment, film and developing, shipping, food, accommodations, tires, airfare, and other things, Pulko estimates the journey cost more than $100,000!

1. If you were to ride a motorcycle around the world, what are the top five countries you would most like to visit?

   1. _____   4. _____

   2. _____   5. _____

   3. _____

2. Finish the sentence.

   Pulko took over _____ **pictures on her journey.**

3. How many days are in five years? How many days are in six years?

   _____

4. If Pulko spent $100,000 over five and a half years, how much did she spend per year? Round to the nearest penny.

   a. $18,181

   b. $18,181.82

   c. $20,000

   d. $15,384.62

5. List the continents that Pulko drove through on her motorcycle journey.

   1. _____   5. _____

   2. _____   6. _____

   3. _____   7. _____

   4. _____

6. What do you think was the most exciting thing Pulko encountered on her trip around the world?

   _____

   _____

Longest Solo Row Across an Ocean

Photo: Guinness World Records Limited

Erden Eruc (Turkey) rowed by himself for 312 days 2 hours from July 10, 2007, to May 17, 2008. He began in California and traveled to Papua New Guinea.

Did You Know?
The row was part of Eruc's project to travel around the world by human power.

ACTIVITIES

1. Did Eruc row for more than a year or less than a year? Circle your answer.

    more than a year   **less than a year**

2. Look at a world map or globe. Papua New Guinea lies just north of what country/continent that begins with A?

    _____

3. What state lies between California and Papua New Guinea in the Pacific Ocean?

    _____

Farthest Distance Walking on Stilts in 24 Hours

photo: Guinness World Records Limited

In 24 hours, Saimaiti Yiming (China) walked on stilts 49.4 mi. (79.6 km) around Shanshan County, Xinjiang, China, in 2003.

Did You Know?
Yiming's stilts measured 28.7 in. (73 cm) from the ground to his ankle.

ACTIVITIES

1. How many miles did Yiming walk each hour? Round to the nearest tenth of a mile.

   _____

2. What area near you would be a good place to walk on stilts? Explain why you chose that place.

   _____

3. How tall would you be with 28-inch stilts added to your height?

   _____

Greatest Distance on a Human-Powered Vehicle in 24 Hours

Photo: Guinness World Records Limited

Greg Kolodziejzyk (Canada) operated a human-powered vehicle a distance of 647 mi. (1,041.24 km) in 24 hours on July 18, 2006.

Did You Know?

Designed for maximum aerodynamic performance, the human-powered vehicle is a bicycle inside a bullet-shaped body called a *fairing*.

ACTIVITIES

1. *Aerodynamics* is the study of how air pushes and pulls on objects. Wind drags on moving objects and slows them down. Smooth shapes and surfaces let air pass over easily, reducing drag. Explain why the human-powered vehicle is shaped like a bullet.

   _____

   _____

2. Bicycle riders go faster when they lean forward and when they wear helmets. Explain why this is true.

   _____

Longest Snowboarding Marathon

Photo: Guinness World Records Limited

Bernhard Mair (Austria) snowboarded for 180 hours 34 minutes at Bad Kleinkirchheim, Austria, in 2004.

Did You Know?

During his marathon, Mair took 456 ski lift rides.

ACTIVITIES

1. Mair snowboarded for about 180 hours. How many days is that? Use a fraction in your answer.

_____

2. Circle each type of *board* you have used.

keyboard	surfboard	checkerboard
dartboard	snowboard	storyboard
skateboard	boogie board	chalkboard

Greatest Distance by Scooter in 24 Hours

Photo: Guinness World Records Limited

The greatest distance covered by a self-propelled push scooter in 24 hours is 161 mi. (269.1 km) by Matheu Parry (UK) at Seedhill Athletics Track, Nelson, Lancashire, England, on June 9–10, 2000.

Did You Know?

Motorized scooters are able to travel 60–70 mi. on one gallon of gasoline. The average gas mileage of a typical car is 21 mi. per gallon.

CHECK THIS OUT!

Matheu Parry (United Kingdom) first began riding scooters in 1996 after graduating college. Rather than go straight into the workforce, he wanted to do something more exciting.

He settled on the idea of completing the journey between the northern and southernmost points of the British mainland. This journey had been completed before on a variety of different vehicles, but Parry wanted to do something different. Then one day, he saw a child riding on a scooter, and that gave him the perfect idea.

During his journey, he raised $4,650 for a charity that helps the homeless. Then, he decided to attempt the 24-hour distance record. In June 2000, he traveled 161 miles on a scooter in 24 hours!

ACTIVITIES

1. If Parry had raised $5 per mile for charity on his 24-hour journey, how much money would he have raised?

   a. $805

   b. $120

   c. $23,250

   d. $300

2. What would be the advantages of driving a motorized scooter versus a car? What would be the disadvantages?

   Advantages: _____

   _____

   Disadvantages: _____

   _____

3. How many months ago did Parry set the record for Greatest Distance by Scooter in 24 Hours?

   _____

4. What do you want to do after you graduate high school?

   _____

5. Imagine that you want to raise money for charity by setting a world record. How would you raise donations? Create a poster advertising your world record and asking people to sponsor you on your attempt.

Farthest Distance Traveled on a Unicycle in 24 Hours

Photo: Guinness World Records Limited

Sam Wakeling (UK) covered 281.85 mi. (453.6 km) on a unicycle in 24 hours at Aberystwyth, Wales, United Kingdom, in 2007.

Did You Know?

Most unicycles have no gears or chains. The pedals directly crank the axle and move the wheel.

ACTIVITIES

1. How many miles did Wakeling ride each hour?

_____

2. Wakeling set his record in 2007. How many years ago was that?

_____

3. Learning to ride a unicycle requires many hours of practice. What have you spent many hours practicing?

_____

Greatest Rowing Distance in 24 Hours (Men's Team)

Photo: Guinness World Records Limited

A team of three German men (Matthias Auer, Christian Klandt, and Olaf Behrend) rowed 163.42 mi. (263 km) in 24 hours in Berlin, Germany, in 2003.

Did You Know?
The team rowed both upstream and downstream.

ACTIVITIES

1. Do you think greater speeds are achieved when rowing upstream or when rowing downstream? Explain your answer.

_____

_____

2. Three friends worked together to set this rowing record. Write about a time you worked with a team to achieve something you would not have been able to do on your own.

_____

_____

Fastest True Circumnavigation by Bicycle (Male)

Photo: Guinness World Records Limited

Starting and finishing in London, United Kingdom, in 2010, Vincent Cox (UK) went around the world by bicycle in 163 days 6 hours 58 minutes, cycling a distance of 18,225.7 mi. (29,331.48 km).

Did You Know?

Cox cycled through Europe, North Africa, India, Thailand, Malaysia, Singapore, Indonesia, Australia, and the United States.

ACTIVITIES

1. Which is faster—traveling around the world by bicycle or by helicopter (page 151)?

   _____

2. Look at a world map or globe. Write the names of six countries you would like to visit during a trip around the world.

   _____   _____   _____

   _____   _____   _____

Farthest Distance by Canoe/Kayak on Flat Water in 24 Hours (Female)

Photo: Guinness World Records Limited

Robyn Benincasa (USA) piloted a kayak for 24 hours in flat water on Lake San Antonio, California, in 2010. She traveled 121.37 mi. (195.33 km).

Did You Know?
The name *kayak* comes from the Inuit word *qayaq*.

ACTIVITIES

1. How many miles did Benincasa travel each hour?

   _____

2. Look at your answer to #1 on page 174. How many miles per hour faster is it to unicycle for 24 hours than it is to kayak on flat water for 24 hours?

   _____

3. Write the name of a lake that is close to your home.

   _____

Farthest Distance Static Cycling in One Hour (Female)

Photo: Guinness World Records Limited

The greatest distance on a static cycle in one hour by a female is 17.3 mi. (27.84 km) achieved by Fabienne Müller (Switzerland) in Steinmaur, Switzerland, on June 1, 2008.

Did You Know?

Riding a bike for 15 minutes five to six times per week will help you lose up to 11 pounds a year!

CHECK THIS OUT!

What do you like to do for exercise? There are many different ways to exercise, including biking, running, practicing yoga, playing basketball, and lifting weights, just to name a few.

Fabienne Müller (Switzerland) likes a form of exercise called *static cycling*. In static cycling, you are riding a stationary bike, which means that the bicycle doesn't actually go anywhere. It is fixed to a platform and stays in one place, even when pedaling really fast!

Müller holds the world record for the Farthest Distance Static Cycling in One Hour for Females. She cycled for 17.3 miles in one hour in June 2008. She also set another static cycling record on the same day. She went 201.4 miles in 12 hours, which included her one-hour record.

ACTIVITIES

1. Do you think static cycling is a good form of exercise? Explain why or why not.

_____

2. In Müller's 12-hour world record, what was her average speed in miles per hour? Round to the nearest tenth.

   a. 8.4 mph

   b. 8.8 mph

   c. 17.5 mph

   d. 16.8 mph

3. Look at your answer to #2. Was Müller's average distance in miles per hour over the course of her 12-hour record more or less than the distance she cycled for her one-hour world record? Circle your answer.

   more   **less**

4. What is your favorite way to exercise?

_____

5. Circle five words you read on page 178 to complete the word search. Use the word bank to help you.

biking running yoga basketball weights

I	R	H	M	J	B	A	F	B	H
P	U	V	S	D	U	R	H	A	Y
V	N	U	I	E	T	R	Q	S	K
R	N	U	L	E	E	W	G	K	W
A	I	P	U	L	E	F	R	E	E
A	N	Z	X	V	O	L	V	T	I
Y	G	S	P	B	Y	G	M	B	G
O	Q	B	I	K	I	N	G	A	H
G	V	O	I	E	Y	Q	X	L	T
A	A	W	A	V	D	G	G	L	S

Longest Toenails

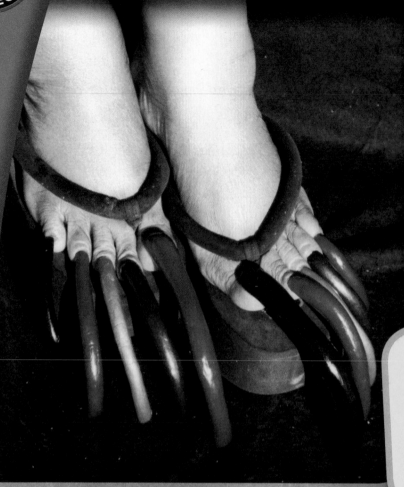

Photo: Guinness World Records Limited

In 1991, Louise Hollis's (USA) toenails were a combined length of 7 ft. 3 in. (2.21 m). She started growing them in 1982.

Did You Know?

Hollis has to wear open-toed shoes with a sole at least 3 in. (7.62 cm) high so her toenails don't drag on the ground.

ACTIVITIES

1. Imagine you are trying to persuade Hollis to cut her toenails. Write two reasons why you think she should cut them.

_____

_____

2. Imagine you are trying to persuade Hollis not to cut her toenails. Write two reasons why you think she should not cut them.

_____

_____

Greatest Karting Distance in 24 Hours Outdoors (Individual)

Photo: Guinness World Records Limited

The greatest distance by kart in 24 hours outdoors is 716.15 mi. (1,152.54 km) and was achieved by Myk Prescott (South Africa) in 2008.

Did You Know?
During his world record attempt, Prescott completed 1,011 laps.

ACTIVITIES

1. How many miles did Prescott travel each hour?

_____

2. What part of a mile was each lap Prescott completed? Round to the nearest hundredth of a mile.

_____

3. Look back at page 170. In 24 hours, how many more total miles did Prescott travel than Kolodziejzyk?

_____

Fastest 10 Kilometer Race While Juggling With Three Objects (Male)

Photo: Guinness World Records Limited

On September 10, 2006, Michal Kapral (Canada) jogged 6.21 mi. (10 km) in 36 minutes 27 seconds while juggling three objects during the Longboat Toronto Island Run, Toronto, Ontario, Canada.

Did You Know?
Kapral not only juggled while jogging, he chewed gum the entire time, too!

ACTIVITIES

1. Can you solve mental math problems, do jumping jacks, and whistle all at the same time? Write three things you can do simultaneously.

   _____   _____   _____

2. Partygoers enjoy watching magicians, jugglers, and other performers. What could you do to entertain people at a party?

   _____

3. What three objects would you like to juggle?

   _____

Most Vertical Ski-Bobbing Distance in 12 Hours (Individual)

Photo: Guinness World Records Limited

The record for the most vertical distance ski-bobbed in 12 hours is 107,401 ft. 4 in. (32,736 m) and is held equally by Harald Brenter and Hermann Koch (both Austria).

Did You Know?
A *ski-bob* is a type of ski-bike, a vehicle mounted on short skis. The rider also wears short skis on his or her feet.

ACTIVITIES

1. What part of a day is 12 hours? Write your answer as a fraction.

   _____

2. Why do you think ski-bobbing is called a *gravity sport*?

   _____

3. Circle downhill sports you enjoy or would like to try.

   sledding   **water sliding**   **skiing**

   snowboarding   **downhill mountain biking**   **ski-bobbing**

Farthest Distance to Pull a Bus With the Hair

Photo: Guinness World Records Limited

On November 11, 2009, Manjit Singh (UK) pulled a double-decker bus a distance of 69.55 ft. (21.2 m) for Guinness World Records Day in Battersea Park, London, United Kingdom.

Did You Know?
The first double-decker buses were pulled by horses.

ACTIVITIES

1. Newton's first law of motion states that objects in motion tend to stay in motion with the same direction and speed. How does this law help explain why Singh was able to pull the double-decker bus?

_____

_____

2. Double-decker buses can be fun to ride. Write the name of a multi-level vehicle you would like to invent.

_____

Smallest Dog Living (Height)

Boo Boo, a long-haired Chihuahua, measured 4 in. (10.16 cm) tall on May 12, 2007. She lives in Raceland, Kentucky.

Did You Know?
Boo Boo was about the size of a thumb when she was born and was fed with an eyedropper every two hours.

ACTIVITIES

1. Boo Boo is four inches tall. What do you own that is about four inches tall? Use a ruler to find out.
   Answers will vary.

2. Chihuahuas get their name from the Mexican state of Chihuahua. English has borrowed many words from Spanish. Can you fill in the English words?

Spanish		English
tornar ("to turn") =	tornado	("a turning storm")
el lagarto ("the lizard") =	alligator	("a large reptile")

6

Largest Rodent

The capybara has a head and body length of 3 ft. 3 in. (99.06 cm) and can weigh up to 174 lb. (79 kg). It is found in Argentina, Uruguay, and Brazil.

Did You Know?
Capybaras can be trained like dogs. A South American blind man trained a capybara as a guide animal.

ACTIVITIES

1. There are 16 ounces in a pound. How many ounces does a 174-pound capybara weigh?
   2,784 ounces

2. A hamster weighs about five ounces. About how many hamsters would it take to weigh as much as a 174-pound capybara? Round to the nearest whole number.
   557 hamsters

3. Name two more rodents. Answers will vary.

7

Longest Ears on a Rabbit

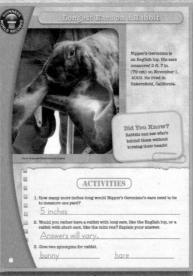

Nipper's Geronimo is an English lop. His ears measured 2 ft. 7 in. (79 cm) on November 1, 2003. He lived in Bakersfield, California.

Did You Know?
Rabbits can see who's behind them without turning their head!

ACTIVITIES

1. How many more inches long would Nipper's Geronimo's ears need to be to measure one yard?
   5 inches

2. Would you rather have a rabbit with long ears, like the English lop, or a rabbit with short ears, like the mini rex? Explain your answer.
   Answers will vary.

3. Give two synonyms for rabbit.
   bunny   hare

8

Most Dogs Walked Simultaneously by an Individual

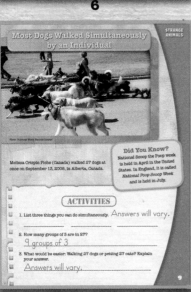

Melissa Crispin Piche (Canada) walked 27 dogs at once on September 13, 2008, in Alberta, Canada.

Did You Know?
National Scoop the Poop week is held in April in the United States. In England, it is called National Poop Scoop Week and is held in July.

ACTIVITIES

1. List three things you can do simultaneously. Answers will vary.

2. How many groups of 3 are in 27?
   9 groups of 3

3. What would be easier: Walking 27 dogs or petting 27 cats? Explain your answer.
   Answers will vary.

9

ACTIVITIES

1. About how many colors can the mantis shrimp see? Explain how you determined your answer.
   About 100,000 colors. The mantis shrimp sees 10 times more colors than humans, who see 10,000 colors.

2. Finish the sentence.
   Dogs   have ½ as many color receptors as the mantis shrimp.

3. Which Celsius temperature is equal to the temperature that the swordfish can heat its eyes up to?
   a. 0°C
   b. 35°C
   c. 55°C
   d. 100°C

4. Fill in the table with information you read on page 10. If the information cannot be determined from the passage, write N/A.

Animal	Number of Receptors	Colors That Are Visible
Humans	3	10,000
Dogs	2	N/A
Mantis Shrimp	8	100,000

5. Look around your room. How many different colors can you see? Circle your answer. Answers will vary.
   more than 50   less than 50

6. With an adult, find several different shades of paint. Mix two paint colors together to form new colors. Give each new color you create a name. List them here.
   Answers will vary.

11

Fastest Eater (Mammals)

The star-nosed mole can identify food, capture it, and eat it in an average "handling time" of 230 milliseconds, with the fastest time being 120 milliseconds.

Did You Know?
The star-nosed mole has 22 pink tentacles that form the star on its nose. Its tentacles can also detect food under water.

ACTIVITIES

1. There are 1,000 milliseconds in one second. It takes you about 100 milliseconds to blink. About how many times could you blink in the time it takes an average star-nosed mole to eat?
   2 times

2. Most living creatures have the same number of body parts on each side. Due to this quality, how many tentacles does the star-nosed mole have on each side of its amazing nose?
   11 tentacles on each side

12

Most Celebrated Canine Rescuer

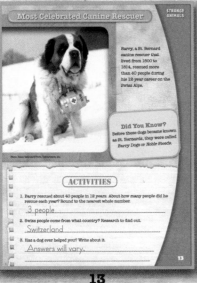

Barry, a St. Bernard canine rescuer that lived from 1800 to 1814, rescued more than 40 people during his 12-year career on the Swiss Alps.

Did You Know?
Before these dogs became known as St. Bernards, they were called Barry Dogs or Noble Steeds.

ACTIVITIES

1. Barry rescued about 40 people in 12 years. About how many people did he rescue each year? Round to the nearest whole number.
   3 people

2. Swiss people come from what country? Research to find out.
   Switzerland

3. Has a dog ever helped you? Write about it.
   Answers will vary.

13

ACTIVITIES

1. Mermaids are real creatures. True or false? Circle your answer.
   true   **false**

2. An animal that uses camouflage for defense
   a. hides behind large objects.
   b. blends in with its surroundings.
   c. shows its teeth or claws.
   d. has no protection against predators.

3. Do you think a seahorse is unusual? Explain why or why not.
   Answers will vary.

4. Name one way seahorses are like other fish.
   Suggested answer: Seahorses live underwater.

5. About how many varieties of seahorses exist?
   a. 50
   b. 25
   c. 30
   d. 45

6. Design a machine that could help seahorses swim faster. Draw it here and explain to a friend how it works.

   Drawings will vary.

17

Most Steps Walked Down by a Dog Facing Forwards Balancing a Glass of Water

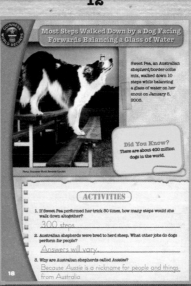

Sweet Pea, an Australian shepherd/border collie mix, walked down 10 steps while balancing a glass of water on her snout on January 5, 2008.

Did You Know?
There are about 400 million dogs in the world.

ACTIVITIES

1. If Sweet Pea performed her trick 30 times, how many steps would she walk down altogether?
   300 steps

2. Australian shepherds were bred to herd sheep. What other jobs do dogs perform for people?
   Answers will vary.

3. Why are Australian shepherds called Aussie?
   Because Aussie is a nickname for people and things from Australia

18

Card 19 — Largest Carnivore on Land

Largest Carnivore on Land

Adult male polar bears weigh about 880-1,320 lb. (400-600 kg). They measure 7 ft. 10 in. to 8 ft. 6 in. (2.4-2.6 m) from nose to tail.

Did You Know?
Polar bears sometimes cover their black noses with their white paws so seals will not see them.

ACTIVITIES

1. Polar bears live along the Arctic Ocean. Describe the position of the Arctic Ocean on planet Earth.
   It is at the top of the planet, above Canada.

2. Would eight 150-pound human adults weigh more or less than the largest polar bear? Circle your answer.
   more   (less)

3. What type of bear lives closest to your home?
   Answers will vary.

19

Card 23

ACTIVITIES

1. How many hands equal one foot?
   3 hands

2. In inches, how much taller is Big Jake than most horses?
   18.7 inches

3. About how tall is Big Jake in feet and inches?
   a. 5 feet, 11 inches
   (b.) 6 feet, 11 inches
   c. 7 feet, 6 inches
   d. 6 feet, 3 inches

4. What is your height in feet and inches? How many hands tall are you?
   Answers will vary.

5. The Tallest Ox measured 6 feet, 5 inches tall. The Tallest Mammal, a giraffe, was 19 feet tall. Order the record-setting animals from 1 to 4, with 1 being shortest and 4 being tallest.

   3 horse
   1 mule
   4 giraffe
   2 ox

6. If a giraffe were measured in hands, how many hands tall would the Tallest Giraffe be?
   57 hands

23

Card 25 — Most Dolphins Born in a Year

Most Dolphins Born in a Year

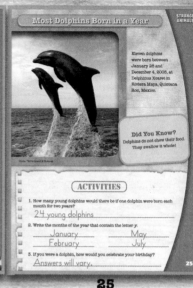

Eleven dolphins were born between January 28 and December 4, 2008, at Delphinus Xcaret in Riviera Maya, Quintana Roo, Mexico.

Did You Know?
Dolphins do not chew their food. They swallow it whole!

ACTIVITIES

1. How many young dolphins would there be if one dolphin were born each month for two years?
   24 young dolphins

2. Write the months of the year that contain the letter y.
   January   May
   February   July

3. If you were a dolphin, how would you celebrate your birthday?
   Answers will vary.

25

Card 26 — Heaviest Spider

Heaviest Spider

Rosi, a female Goliath bird-eating spider, weighed 6.17 oz. (175 g) on July 27, 2007. She lives in Andorf, Austria.

Did You Know?
The Goliath bird-eating spider does not have teeth, but uses its large, inch-long fangs to bite.

ACTIVITIES

1. Does Rosi weigh more or less than one-half pound? Circle your answer.
   more   (less)

2. What do most spiders eat?
   insects

3. Who is Goliath? Why is Rosi's breed of spider called Goliath?
   Goliath is a famous giant warrior. Rosi's type of spider is called goliath because it is so big.

26

Card 27 — Most Tennis Balls Held in the Mouth by a Dog

Most Tennis Balls Held in the Mouth by a Dog

Augie, a golden retriever, held five regulation-sized tennis balls in his mouth on July 6, 2003. He lived in Dallas, Texas.

Did You Know?
Golden retrievers make good service dogs. Service dogs guide blind people, pull wheelchairs, and turn on lights. Some can dial 9-1-1.

ACTIVITIES

1. Estimate how many books, toys, or other items will fit in your backpack. Test your hypothesis. How close was your guess?
   Answers will vary.

2. How many balls would Augie hold in his mouth if he did his trick each day for one week?
   35 balls

3. Why do you think Augie likes tennis balls?
   Answers will vary.

27

Card 29

ACTIVITIES

1. In what way are Komodo dragons and sharks alike?
   a. They both climb trees.
   b. They both use gills to breathe.
   (c.) They both have teeth that are replaced often.
   d. They are gray in color.

2. People have known about Komodo dragons for millions of years. True or false? Circle your answer.
   true   (false)

3. How does the Komodo dragon compare with your idea of dragons from fictional tales? Fill in the Venn diagram to compare and contrast the two creatures.

   Komodo Dragons   Fictional Dragons

   Answers will vary.

4. From the passage on page 28, you can conclude that Komodo dragons are
   (a.) dangerous animals.
   b. slow, lazy creatures.
   c. related to dinosaurs.
   d. small.

5. The dragons use their sharp sense of smell to find prey. What is a synonym for sharp?
   Suggest answers: pointy, prickly, spiky

29

Card 32 — Largest Colony of Mammals

Largest Colony of Mammals

A colony of black-tailed prairie dogs, discovered in 1901, contained about 400 million residents. The "town" covered about 23,706 sq. mi. (61,400 km²), almost the size of Ireland.

Did You Know?
Prairie dogs seem to kiss each other when they meet, although they're really just touching their teeth together.

ACTIVITIES

1. A square mile is an area of land shaped like a square. How many feet long is a square mile on each of its four sides?
   One mile

2. Prairie dogs live underground in connected tunnels. Draw a prairie dog town.
   Drawings will vary.

32

Card 33 — Largest Horn Circumference on a Steer

Largest Horn Circumference on a Steer

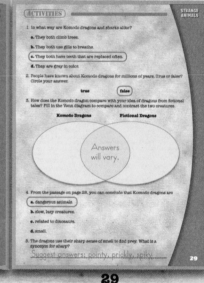

Lurch's horns measured 37.5 in. (95.25 cm) in circumference on May 6, 2003. His horn span was about 8 ft. 10.6 in. (2.1 m) long. Lurch is an African Watusi steer and lives in Gassville, Arkansas.

Did You Know?
Ofila, a longhorn steer, lives on President George W. Bush's ranch with her calves Ellie and Logan. All were named after former staff members.

ACTIVITIES

1. Circumference measures the distance around a circle. What is the circumference of your wrist in inches? Use a tape measure to find out.
   Answers will vary.

2. Measure this line in inches.
   4 inches

3. If the line you measured became a circle, what would be its circumference?
   4 inches

33

Card 35

ACTIVITIES

1. How old will Midge be in 2016?
   20 years old

2. Midge's tail is about what fraction of the length of her body?
   a. ⅛ of her body
   b. ⅓ of her body
   (c.) ½ of her body
   d. ¼ of her body

3. Using a ruler, draw a picture of Midge to scale. Use this scale: ⅛ of an inch equals one inch.

   Drawing should show a dog 11/16 of an inch tall and 1 inch long with the tail 7/16 inches long.

4. What are two ways that Midge's size helps her to sniff out drugs?
   1. She can search in cars.
   2. She can search in school lockers.

5. The Most Successful Sniffer Dog is Snag, a Labrador retriever. He has made 118 drug recoveries with a total cost of $810,000,000. What is $810,000,000 divided by 118? Round your answer to the nearest hundredth.
   $6,864,406.78

6. What is the capital of Ohio? How many other cities can you name that begin with the same letter as Ohio's capital?
   Columbus; Answers will vary.

35

Longest Tongue on a Dog

STRANGE ANIMALS

Puggy, a Pekingese, has a tongue that measured 4.5 in. (11.43 cm) on May 8, 2009. Puggy lives in Bedford, Texas.

Did You Know?
Dog nose prints are unique and can identify a dog like fingerprints can identify a human.

ACTIVITIES

1. How long is your tongue? Use a ruler to find out.
   Answers will vary.
2. Write the length of Puggy's tongue as a fraction.
   4½ inches
3. The Pekingese is a small, muscular dog with shaggy fur and a proud personality. Describe your pet or a pet you would like to have.
   Answers will vary.

37

Oldest Kinkajou in Captivity

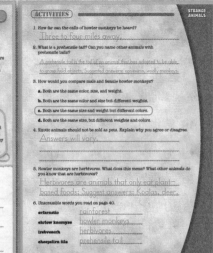

Huggy Bear was 27 years and 6 months old in January 2004. He lives in Holiday, Florida.

Did You Know?
Kinkajous are sometimes called honey bears because they raid bees' nests. They slurp the honey with long, skinny tongues.

ACTIVITIES

1. Huggy Bear was 27 in 2004. In what year will he be 40?
   The year 2017
2. In what year will you be 20 years old?
   Answers will vary.
3. Unlike wild animals, animals in captivity live with humans. List some places you might find wild and captive animals.
   wild animals: forest, fields, lakes
   captive animals: zoos, farms, people's houses

38

ACTIVITIES

STRANGE ANIMALS

1. How far can the calls of howler monkeys be heard?
   Three to four miles away.
2. What is a prehensile tail? Can you name other animals with prehensile tails?
   A prehensile tail is the tail of an animal that has adapted to be able to grasp held objects. Suggested answers: opossums, wooly monkeys.
3. How would you compare male and female howler monkeys?
   a. Both are the same color, size, and weight.
   b. Both are the same color and size but different weights.
   c. Both are the same size and weight but different colors.
   d. Both are the same size, but different weights and colors.
4. Exotic animals should not be sold as pets. Explain why you agree or disagree.
   Answers will vary.
5. Howler monkeys are herbivores. What does that mean? What other animals do you know that are herbivores?
   Herbivores are animals that only eat plant-based foods. Suggest answers: Koalas, deer.
6. Unscramble words you read on page 40.
   erfarnstio — rainforest
   ehrlow knomyse — howler monkeys
   irebveeorh — herbivores
   cheepsilrn ilta — prehensile tail

41

Highest Jump by a Pig

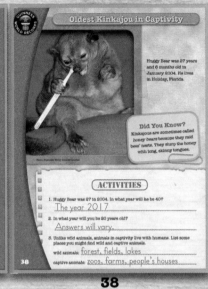

Kotetsu, a potbellied pig, jumped 2 ft. 3.5 in. (70 cm) high on August 22, 2004, at a farm in Mie, Japan.

Did You Know?
Potbellied pigs rarely weigh over 180 lb. (66 kg). They are popular pets because they are smaller than farm pigs and can be housebroken.

ACTIVITIES

1. Kotetsu jumped 2 feet, 3.5 inches. How many inches is that in all?
   27.5 inches
2. Use tape to mark a start line on the floor and a finish line two feet, four inches away. How many hops or jumps does it take you to get from one line to the other?
   Answers will vary.
3. Would you like a pig for a pet? Explain your answer.
   Answers will vary.

42

Most Expensive Painting by Elephants

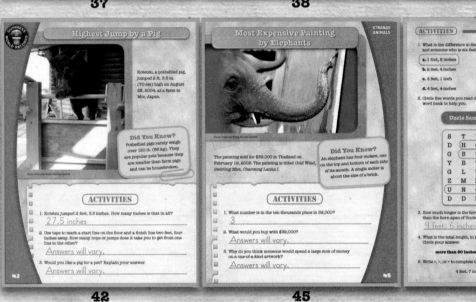

The painting sold for $39,000 in Thailand on February 19, 2005. The painting is titled *Cold Wind, Swirling Mist, Charming Lanna I.*

Did You Know?
An elephant has four molars, one on the top and bottom of each side of its mouth. A single molar is about the size of a brick.

ACTIVITIES

1. What number is in the ten-thousands place in 39,000?
   3
2. What would you buy with $39,000?
   Answers will vary.
3. Why do you think someone would spend a large sum of money on a one-of-a-kind artwork?
   Answers will vary.

45

ACTIVITIES

STRANGE ANIMALS

1. What is the difference in feet and inches between Uncle Sam's horn span and someone who is six feet tall?
   a. 1 foot, 6 inches
   b. 2 feet, 4 inches
   c. 4 feet, 1 inch
   d. 4 feet, 4 inches
2. Circle five words you read on page 46 to complete the word search. Use the word bank to help you.

Uncle Sam   goat   bull   buffalo   horns

S	T	V	B	R	C	C	R
D	H	O	R	N	S	Y	P
G	B	U	F	F	A	L	O
Y	B	T	B	B	L	L	S
G	L	U	U	G	O	A	T
Z	M	H	L	C	V	H	Z
U	N	C	L	E	S	A	M
D	D	H	P	S	Y	S	O

3. How much longer is the horn span from tip to tip of the Asian water buffalo than the horn span of Uncle Sam?
   9 feet, 6 inches
4. What is the total length, in inches, of Uncle Sam's left and right horns? Circle your answer.
   more than 80 inches   **less than 80 inches**
5. Write <, >, or = to complete the equation.
   4 feet, 7 inches > 52 inches

47

Longest Goldfish

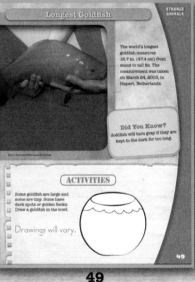

STRANGE ANIMALS

The world's longest goldfish measures 18.7 in. (47.4 cm) from snout to tail fin. The measurement was taken on March 24, 2003, in Hapert, Netherlands.

Did You Know?
Goldfish will turn gray if they are kept in the dark for too long.

ACTIVITIES

Some goldfish are large and some are tiny. Some have dark spots or golden flecks. Draw a goldfish in the bowl.
Drawings will vary.

49

ACTIVITIES

STRANGE ANIMALS

1. What adjective would best describe Anastasia?
   a. lonely
   b. heavy
   c. energetic
   d. bored
2. Finish the sentence.
   Anastasia pops balloons by biting them.
3. Using only your hands, how many balloons can you pop in 60 seconds?
   Answers will vary.
4. Why might helium-filled balloons be more difficult to use when breaking a world record?
   Suggested answer: Helium balloons would float to the ceiling.
5. Balloons can come in all different shapes and colors. Decorate these balloons any way you like. Drawings will vary.

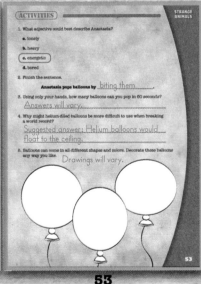

53

Largest Mouth of All Land Animals

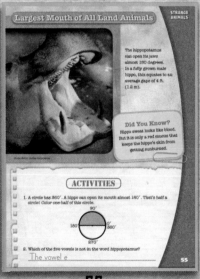

STRANGE ANIMALS

The hippopotamus can open its jaws almost 180 degrees. In a fully grown male hippo, this equates to an average gape of 4 ft. (1.2 m).

Did You Know?
Hippo sweat looks like blood. But it is only a red mucus that keeps the hippo's skin from getting sunburned.

ACTIVITIES

1. A circle has 360°. A hippo can open its mouth almost 180°. That's half a circle! Color one-half of this circle.
2. Which of the five vowels is not in the word *hippopotamus*?
   The vowel e

55

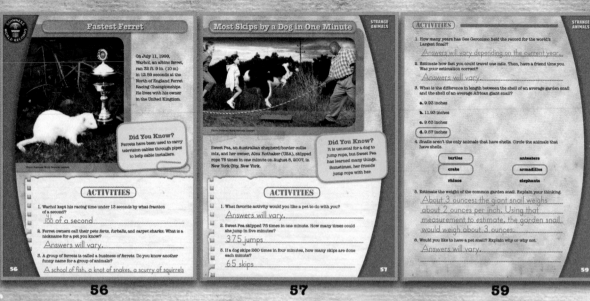

Fastest Ferret

On July 11, 1999, Warhol, an albino ferret, ran 32 ft. 9 in. (10 m) in 12.59 seconds at the North of England Ferret Racing Championships. He lives with his owner in the United Kingdom.

Did You Know?
Ferrets have been used to carry television cables through pipes to help cable installers.

ACTIVITIES

1. Warhol kept his racing time under 13 seconds by what fraction of a second?
   100 of a second

2. Ferret owners call their pets ferts, furballs, and carpet sharks. What is a nickname for a pet you know?
   Answers will vary.

3. A group of ferrets is called a business of ferrets. Do you know another funny name for a group of animals?
   A school of fish, a knot of snakes, a scurry of squirrels

56

Most Skips by a Dog in One Minute

STRANGE ANIMALS

Sweet Pea, an Australian shepherd/border collie mix, and her owner, Alex Rothaker (USA), skipped rope 75 times in one minute on August 8, 2007, in New York City, New York.

Did You Know?
It is unusual for a dog to jump rope, but Sweet Pea has learned many things. Sometimes, her friends jump rope with her.

ACTIVITIES

1. What favorite activity would you like a pet to do with you?
   Answers will vary.

2. Sweet Pea skipped 75 times in one minute. How many times could she jump in five minutes?
   375 jumps

3. If a dog skips 260 times in four minutes, how many skips are done each minute?
   65 skips

57

ACTIVITIES

STRANGE ANIMALS

1. How many years has Gee Geronimo held the record for the world's Largest Snail?
   Answers will vary depending on the current year.

2. Estimate how fast you could travel one mile. Then, have a friend time you. Was your estimation correct?
   Answers will vary.

3. What is the difference in length between the shell of an average garden snail and the shell of an average African giant snail?
   a. 9.93 inches
   b. 11.93 inches
   c. 9.63 inches
   d. 9.67 inches

4. Snails aren't the only animals that have shells. Circle the animals that have shells.
   turtles   anteaters
   crabs   armadillos
   rhinos   elephants

5. Estimate the weight of the common garden snail. Explain your thinking.
   About 3 ounces; the giant snail weighs about 2 ounces per inch. Using that measurement to estimate, the garden snail would weigh about 3 ounces.

6. Would you like to have a pet snail? Explain why or why not.
   Answers will vary.

59

Longest Tail on a Pony

On March 28, 2008, Delies Babe Romper, a miniature stallion, had a tail that measured 8 ft. 6 in. (2.59 m) at a farm in Litchfield, Minnesota.

Did You Know?
Before a horse falls asleep on its feet, it locks its back legs so it will not fall over!

ACTIVITIES

1. What is the length of Delies Babe Romper's tail in inches?
   102 inches

2. What animal would you like to own in a miniature version?
   Answers will vary.

3. How long is your hair? Use a ruler or tape measure to find out.
   Answers will vary.

60

Largest Millipede

The largest millipede in the world is an African giant black millipede. It measures 15.2 in. (38.7 cm) in length, 2.6 in. (6.7 cm) in circumference, and has 256 legs.

Did You Know?
Millipedes breathe through small holes located on the sides of their bodies.

ACTIVITIES

1. The prefix milli- means "thousand." How do you think the millipede got its name?
   It got its name because it has so many legs, it may seem like 1,000 legs, though the number is actually fewer.

2. Use paper, clay, or foil to make a model of a 15-inch-long millipede. Tell what you did.
   Answers will vary.

3. How many legs does the African giant black millipede have on each side?
   128 legs

61

Tallest Mammal

Adult male giraffes measure between 15 and 18 ft. (4.6-5.5 m) tall. Giraffes are found in the dry savannah and open woodland areas of sub-Saharan Africa.

Did You Know?
A giraffe's tongue can grow to be 18-20 in. (46-51 cm) long, about as long as your arm.

ACTIVITIES

1. A one-story building is about 10 feet tall. About how many stories tall is a male giraffe?
   1½ stories

2. What would you do today if you were as tall as a giraffe?
   Answers will vary.

3. The Sahara Desert divides the continent of Africa. Write the name of a country in sub-Saharan Africa.
   Suggested answer: Botswana

62

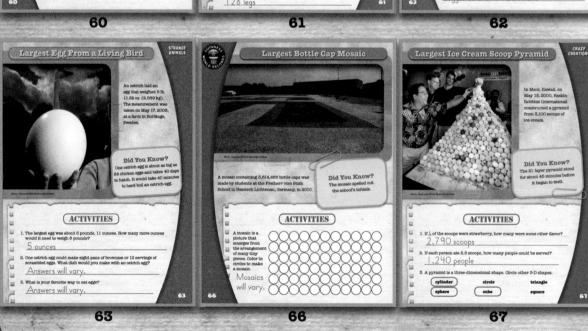

Largest Egg From a Living Bird

STRANGE ANIMALS

An ostrich laid an egg that weighed 5 lb. 11.32 oz. (2.589 kg). The measurement was taken on May 17, 2008, at a farm in Borlänge, Sweden.

Did You Know?
One ostrich egg is about as big as 24 chicken eggs and takes 40 days to hatch. It would take 40 minutes to hard-boil an ostrich egg.

ACTIVITIES

1. The largest egg was about 5 pounds, 11 ounces. How many more ounces would it need to weigh 6 pounds?
   5 ounces

2. One ostrich egg could make eight pans of brownies or 12 servings of scrambled eggs. What dish would you make with an ostrich egg?
   Answers will vary.

3. What is your favorite way to eat eggs?
   Answers will vary.

63

Largest Bottle Cap Mosaic

A mosaic containing 3,614,465 bottle caps was made by students at the Freiherr vom Stein School in Hessisch Lichtenau, Germany, in 2010.

Did You Know?
The mosaic spelled out the school's initials.

ACTIVITIES

A mosaic is a picture that emerges from the arrangement of many tiny pieces. Color in circles to make a mosaic.
Mosaics will vary.

66

Largest Ice Cream Scoop Pyramid

CRAZY CREATIONS

In Maui, Hawaii, on May 18, 2000, Baskin-Robbins International constructed a pyramid from 3,100 scoops of ice cream.

Did You Know?
The 21-layer pyramid stood for about 45 minutes before it began to melt.

ACTIVITIES

1. If ⅒ of the scoops were strawberry, how many were some other flavor?
   2,790 scoops

2. If each person ate 2.5 scoops, how many people could be served?
   1,240 people

3. A pyramid is a three-dimensional shape. Circle other 3-D shapes.
   cylinder   circle   triangle
   sphere   cube   square

67

Most Henna Tattoos Completed in an Hour

CRAZY CREATIONS

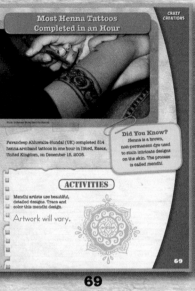

Pavandeep Ahluwalia-Hundal (UK) completed 314 henna armband tattoos in one hour in Ilford, Essex, United Kingdom, on December 13, 2008.

Did You Know? Henna is a brown, non-permanent dye used to stain intricate designs on the skin. The process is called mendhi.

ACTIVITIES

Mendhi artists use beautiful, detailed designs. Trace and color this mendhi design.

Artwork will vary.

69

ACTIVITIES

CRAZY CREATIONS

1. The area of this shape is 441 square feet. If each side is the same length, what is the length of each side?

A = 441 sq. ft.   L = __21 ft.__

2. Find several toothpicks. What interesting shape or design can you make using only toothpicks? Draw it here.

Drawings will vary.

3. In what school-wide event have you participated?
   __Answers will vary.__

4. If toothpicks come in boxes of 100, how many boxes of toothpicks were needed for the mosaic? Round to the nearest tenth.
   a. 16,208.4 boxes
   b. 16,208 boxes
   c. 1,620.84 boxes
   d. 162,084 boxes

5. How many students would Yaugeno High School have if enrollment doubled? Circle your answer.
   more than 800   less than 800

71

Longest Model Train

CRAZY CREATIONS

A model train measuring 892 ft. 3 in. (271.97 m) long was built by Miniature Wunderland GmbH in an arena in Hamburg, Germany, in 2008.

Did You Know? The train included eight engines and 3,312 cars.

ACTIVITIES

1. About how many cars were pulled by each engine? Round to the nearest whole number.
   __277 cars__

2. Some people collect miniature animal figurines, football helmets, or airplanes. Describe a miniature you own.
   __Answers will vary.__

3. What is frequently transported by train?
   __Suggested answers: coal, lumber, oil, vehicles__

73

Largest Painting by Numbers

Ecole de Demin, a school in Lagos State, Nigeria, unveiled a paint-by-numbers artwork with an area of 33,696 sq. ft. 160.2 sq. in. (3,130.86 m²) on November 17, 2010.

Did You Know? The painting depicted the map and flag of Nigeria.

ACTIVITIES

1. There are more than 50 countries on the African continent. Look at a map. Write the name of a third nation for each region.   Suggested answers:
   North Africa: Libya, Algeria, __Egypt__
   West Africa: Nigeria, Senegal, __Cameroon__
   East Africa: Ethiopia, Eritrea, __Somalia__
   South Africa: Namibia, Mozambique, __South Africa__

2. Write the name of the African country you would most like to visit.
   __Answers will vary.__

74

Largest Model of a Human Organ

CRAZY CREATIONS

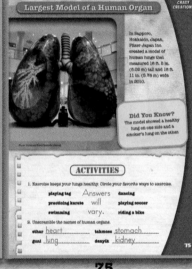

In Sapporo, Hokkaido, Japan, Pfizer Japan Inc. created a model of human lungs that measured 18 ft. 3 in. (5.02 m) tall and 18 ft. 11 in. (5.76 m) wide in 2010.

Did You Know? The model showed a healthy lung on one side and a smoker's lung on the other.

ACTIVITIES

1. Exercise keeps your lungs healthy. Circle your favorite ways to exercise.

   playing tag   Answers   dancing
   practicing karate   will   playing soccer
   swimming   vary.   riding a bike

2. Unscramble the names of human organs.
   ethar __heart__   tshmoac __stomach__
   guni __lung__   denyik __kidney__

75

ACTIVITIES

CRAZY CREATIONS

1. If 600 students were in charge of assembling the same number of friendship bracelets, how many was each student in charge of? Round to the nearest hundredth.
   a. 6.3 bracelets
   b. 6.53 bracelets
   c. 3.66 bracelets
   d. 3.7 bracelets

2. Finish the sentence.
   The idea for the bracelet came about after Owingsville Elementary School hosted a __Friendship Day__ .

3. Is 810 feet more or less than a quarter-mile? Circle your answer.
   more   less

4. Create a chain using strips of construction paper and glue or tape. Take a strip of paper and glue or tape both ends together so that it forms a circle. Then, take another strip of paper and link it through the circle before gluing its ends together. Continue the chain until you run out of paper. How long is your chain?
   __Answers will vary.__

5. What are three adjectives you can use to describe your best friend?
   __Answers will vary.__

6. Think of something you could give a friend as a symbol of your friendship. Draw it here.

Drawings will vary.

77

Fastest Marathon by a Marching Band

Twenty members of the Huddersfield University Marching Band (UK) completed a marathon in 7 hours 55 minutes while playing their instruments in London, United Kingdom, on April 17, 2011.

Did You Know? The Rose Parade happens in Pasadena, California, every January. Many of the nation's best marching bands are invited each year.

ACTIVITIES

1. How many minutes did it take the band to complete the marathon?
   __475 minutes__

2. There are about 26 miles in a marathon. About what part of a mile did the band complete each minute?
   __0.05 miles__

3. How many fewer minutes would make the band's marathon time an hour?
   __115 minutes__

78

Largest Underwater Painting

CRAZY CREATIONS

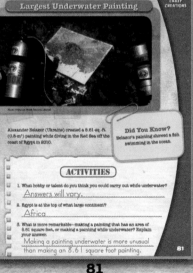

Alexander Belozor (Ukraine) created a 8.61-sq.-ft. (0.8 m²) painting while diving in the Red Sea off the coast of Egypt in 2010.

Did You Know? Belozor's painting showed a fish swimming in the ocean.

ACTIVITIES

1. What hobby or talent do you think you could carry out while underwater?
   __Answers will vary.__

2. Egypt is at the top of what large continent?
   __Africa__

3. What is more remarkable—making a painting that has an area of 8.61 square feet, or making a painting while underwater? Explain your answer.
   __Making a painting underwater is more unusual than making an 8.61 square foot painting.__

81

ACTIVITIES

CRAZY CREATIONS

1. Think of the best birthday present you've ever given someone. How did that person react? How did it make you feel?
   __Answers will vary.__

2. Use three adjectives to describe the Largest Toast Mosaic.   suggested answers:
   __large__   __brown__   __unique__

3. What would you do if you were able to hang out with 40 of your closest friends?
   __Answers will vary.__

4. Ask an adult to make two pieces of toast. Using only your teeth, bite the toast into different shapes and sizes. What does your toast creation look like? Draw it here.

Drawings will vary.

5. If Hadland used 600 loaves of bread in her toast mosaic, how many slices of bread were there in each loaf? Round to the nearest hundredth.
   a. 16.4 slices
   b. 26.4 slices
   c. 26.42 slices
   d. 16.42 slices

6. Finish the sentence.
   Hadland is __23__ years younger than her mother-in-law.

83

Largest Rocking Horse

On September 12, 2010, Ofer Mor (Israel) finished building a rocking horse that was 24 ft. 11 in. (7.6 m) long and 20 ft. (6.10 m) tall.

Did You Know?
There is evidence that children in ancient Greece and Egypt played with toy horses on wheels.

ACTIVITIES

1. Each floor, or story, of a building is about 10 feet tall. How many stories tall is the Largest Rocking Horse?
   2½ stories

2. Would you rather ride on the Largest Rocking Horse or explore the Largest Cardboard Box Sculpture (page 66)? Explain your answer.
   Answers will vary.

84

CRAZY CREATIONS

Largest Button Mosaic

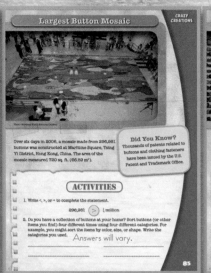

Over six days in 2006, a mosaic made from 296,981 buttons was constructed at Maritime Square, Tsing Yi District, Hong Kong, China. The area of the mosaic measured 720 sq. ft. (66.89 m²).

Did You Know?
Thousands of patents related to buttons and clothing fasteners have been issued by the U.S. Patent and Trademark Office.

ACTIVITIES

1. Write <, >, or = to complete the statement.
   296,981 $>$ ¼ million

2. Do you have a collection of buttons at your home? Sort buttons (or other items you find) four different times using four different categories. For example, you might sort the items by color, size, or shape. Write the categories you used.
   Answers will vary.

85

CRAZY CREATIONS

Largest Collection of Apples

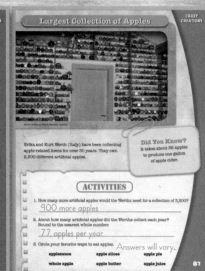

Erika and Kurt Werth (Italy) have been collecting apple-related items for over 30 years. They own 2,500 different artificial apples.

Did You Know?
It takes about 36 apples to produce one gallon of apple cider.

ACTIVITIES

1. How many more artificial apples would the Werths need for a collection of 3,200?
   900 more apples

2. About how many artificial apples did the Werths collect each year? Round to the nearest whole number.
   77 apples per year

3. Circle your favorite ways to eat apples. Answers will vary.
   applesauce   apple slices   apple pie
   whole apple   apple butter   apple juice

87

ACTIVITIES

1. Trace your hand on a piece of paper. Then, trace your friend's hand. Whose hand is bigger?
   Answers will vary.

2. Find eight blank pieces of paper that are all the same size. Draw a picture on each piece, and then combine the sheets of paper into one big drawing. How big is the final work of art?
   Answers will vary.

3. Create your own drawing that promotes tolerance for people that are different in society.

   Drawings will vary.

4. In feet and inches, how long were the eight pieces of fabric used in the Largest Handprint Painting?
   a. 261 feet
   b. 261 feet, 3 inches
   c. 18 feet
   d. 18 feet, 6 inches

5. When was the last time you lent a hand to help someone? What did you do and how did it make you feel?
   Answers will vary.

89

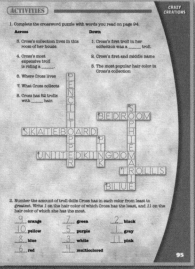

Largest Puppet/Marionette

The mascot for the Ital-Fest in Ottawa, Canada, in 2008, was a marionette that measured 56 ft. 5.5 in. (17 m 82 cm) tall.

Did You Know?
The Ital-Fest celebrates Canadian-Italian heritage. Red, green, and white are the colors of the Italian flag.

ACTIVITIES

1. An oak tree is about 50–60 feet tall. Is the Largest Puppet/Marionette about the same height as an oak tree? Circle your answer.
   yes   no

2. Look at a map. What large ocean lies between Europe (where Italy is found) and North America (where Canada is found)?
   The Atlantic Ocean

3. What states would you need to travel through to reach Canada from your home?
   Answers will vary.

90

Largest Serving of Meatballs

On May 24, 2009, a serving of meatballs weighing 689 lb. (312.5 kg) was made in Serres, Greece. The meatballs were made with buffalo meat, buffalo milk, parsley, spices, breadcrumbs, and onions.

Did You Know?
In Norway, meatballs are called meat cakes and are served with boiled potatoes, gravy, jam, and stewed green peas.

ACTIVITIES

1. If each meatball weighed ⅛ pound, how many individual meatballs would be in the Largest Serving of Meatballs?
   5,512 meatballs

2. To make meatballs, a meat mixture is usually shaped by hand into round balls. List other foods that are round. Suggested answers:
   doughnut holes   pies   oranges
   pizzas   kiwis   radishes

92

CRAZY CREATIONS

Largest Seashell Mosaic

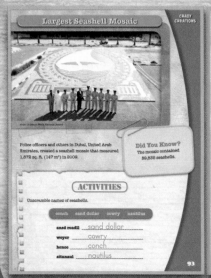

Police officers and others in Dubai, United Arab Emirates, created a seashell mosaic that measured 1,572 sq. ft. (147 m²) in 2009.

Did You Know?
The mosaic contained 89,535 seashells.

ACTIVITIES

Unscramble names of seashells.

conch   sand dollar   cowry   nautilus

snad rodll   sand dollar
woyer   cowry
hcno   conch
situnaul   nautilus

93

CRAZY CREATIONS

ACTIVITIES

1. Complete the crossword puzzle with words you read on page 94.

Across
3. Cross's collection lives in this room of her house.
4. Cross's most expensive troll is riding a _____.
6. Where Cross lives
7. What Cross collects
8. Cross has 52 trolls with _____ hair.

Down
1. Cross's first troll in her collection was a _____ troll.
2. Cross's first and middle name
5. The most popular hair color in Cross's collection

Crossword answers:
- PENCIL
- BEDROOM
- SKATEBOARD
- PINK
- UNITEDKINGDOM
- TROLLS
- BLUE

2. Number the amount of troll dolls Cross has in each color from least to greatest. Write 1 on the hair color of which Cross has the least, and 11 on the hair color of which she has the most.
   9 orange   7 green   2 black
   10 yellow   5 purple   1 gray
   8 blue   3 white   11 pink
   6 red   4 multicolored

95

Largest Horseshoe Sculpture

Donnie Faulk (USA) created a sculpture from 1,071 horseshoes in Pulaski, Tennessee, in 2006.

Did You Know?
Horseshoe crabs were once called horsefoot crabs because their shells resemble a horse's hoof.

ACTIVITIES

1. A hink pink is a riddle made from rhyming words. Write a word that relates to horses to solve each hink pink clue.
   feet seat stirrup   mare chair saddle
   horse course trail   crude food hay

2. If 40 horseshoes were used to make each one of the horse's legs, how many horseshoes were used to create the rest of the horse's body?
   911 horseshoes

96

Longest Painting

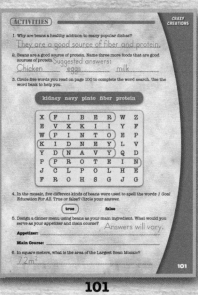

On May 28, 2010, 3,000 students in San Luis Potosí, Mexico, created a painting that measured 19,689 ft. 11 in. (6,001.6 m) long.

Did You Know?
The painting was done on paper and was all about Mexico, its government, and its people.

ACTIVITIES

1. There are 5,280 feet in a mile. About how many miles long was the Longest Painting? Round to the nearest tenth.
   3.7 miles long

2. Would you rather create a giant artwork by yourself (like Tommes Nentwig, page 97) or with a group? Explain your answer.
   Answers will vary.

98

CRAZY CREATIONS

ACTIVITIES

1. Why are beans a healthy addition to many popular dishes?
   They are a good source of fiber and protein.

2. Beans are a good source of protein. Name three more foods that are good sources of protein. Suggested answers:
   Chicken   eggs   milk

3. Circle five words you read on page 100 to complete the word search. Use the word bank to help you.

kidney   navy   pinto   fiber   protein

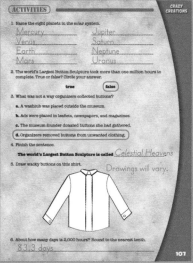

4. In the mosaic, five different kinds of beans were used to spell the words *1 Goal Education For All.* True or false? Circle your answer.
   true   false

5. Design a dinner menu using beans as your main ingredient. What would you serve as your appetizer and main course? **Answers will vary.**

   Appetizer: _____
   Main Course: _____

6. In square meters, what is the area of the Largest Bean Mosaic?
   7.2m²

101

Largest Awareness Ribbon Made With Flowers

CRAZY CREATIONS

An awareness ribbon made of flowers was created on behalf of the Dubai Healthcare City to raise awareness for breast cancer research. It was unveiled on November 16, 2007. It was 94 ft. 2 in. (28.71 m) long and was made out of 105,000 pink carnations.

Did You Know?
Anna Jarvis founded Mother's Day in 1908 and started the tradition of giving out white carnations to mothers everywhere.

ACTIVITIES

1. Write 0 in each space to complete the number of carnations used in the awareness ribbon.
   1 0 5 , 0 0 0

2. How many years ago was 1908? **Answers will vary depending on current year.**

3. Where do you think the Dubai Healthcare City is located? Explain your answer.
   United Arab Emirates, because Dubai is a city in the United Arab Emirates.

103

Largest Cork Mosaic

In 2008, Saimir Strati (Albania) created a mosaic from 229,675 bottle corks at a hotel in Tirana, Albania.

Did You Know?
Strati also holds the record for the Largest Nail Mosaic.

ACTIVITIES

1. About how many bottle corks did the artist use in each quadrant of the mosaic? Round to the nearest whole number.
   57,419 bottle corks

2. With a friend, make a mosaic from squares of colored paper, game pieces, coins, blocks, or other small objects. Explain what you did.
   Answers will vary.

104

CRAZY CREATIONS

ACTIVITIES

1. Name the eight planets in the solar system.
   Mercury   Jupiter
   Venus   Saturn
   Earth   Neptune
   Mars   Uranus

2. The world's Largest Button Sculpture took more than one million hours to complete. True or false? Circle your answer.
   true   **false**

3. What was not a way organizers collected buttons?
   a. A washtub was placed outside the museum.
   b. Ads were placed in leaflets, newspapers, and magazines.
   c. The museum founder donated buttons she had gathered.
   d. Organizers removed buttons from unwanted clothing.

4. Finish the sentence.
   The world's Largest Button Sculpture is called *Celestial Heavens*

5. Draw wacky buttons on this shirt.   **Drawings will vary.**

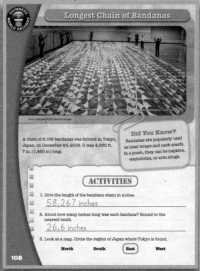

6. About how many days is 2,000 hours? Round to the nearest tenth.
   83.3 days

107

Longest Chain of Bandanas

A chain of 2,155 bandanas was formed in Tokyo, Japan, on December 24, 2009. It was 4,855 ft. 7 in. (1,480 m) long.

Did You Know?
Bandanas are popularly used as head wraps and neck scarfs. In a pinch, they can be napkins, washcloths, or arm slings.

ACTIVITIES

1. Give the length of the bandana chain in inches.
   58,267 inches

2. About how many inches long was each bandana? Round to the nearest tenth.
   26.6 inches

3. Look at a map. Circle the region of Japan where Tokyo is found.
   North   South   **East**   West

108

Largest Pencil Mosaic

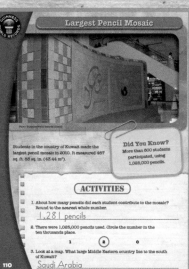

Students in the country of Kuwait made the largest pencil mosaic in 2010. It measured 467 sq. ft. 52 sq. in. (43.44 m²).

Did You Know?
More than 800 students participated, using 1,025,000 pencils.

ACTIVITIES

1. About how many pencils did each student contribute to the mosaic? Round to the nearest whole number.
   1,281 pencils

2. There were 1,025,000 pencils used. Circle the number in the ten thousands place.
   1   **2**   0

3. Look at a map. What large Middle Eastern country lies to the south of Kuwait?
   Saudi Arabia

110

CRAZY CREATIONS

ACTIVITIES

1. Go through your closet and pull out old T-shirts that you haven't worn in a year or longer. What creative way can you reuse them?
   Answers will vary.

2. Go to a store that sells clothing and estimate how many shirts they have for sale. Do you estimate that it's more or less than 2,070 shirts? Circle your answer. **Answers will vary.**
   more   less

3. Would you have wanted to buy one of the limited-edition shirts? Explain why or why not.
   Answers will vary.

4. The shirt mosaic was over 52 feet tall and over 33 feet wide. Was it taller or shorter than a 10-story building? Circle your answer.
   taller   **shorter**

5. If the mosaic used 2,070 shirts in 24 different colors, about how many shirts were used of each color? Round to the nearest hundredth.
   a. 86.3 shirts
   b. 86.25 shirts
   c. 86.25 shirts
   d. 85.3 shirts

6. Design your own one-of-a-kind shirt.

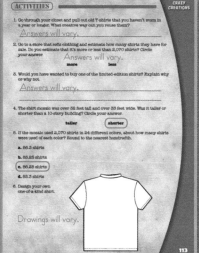

   Drawings will vary.

113

Largest Collection of Converse Shoes

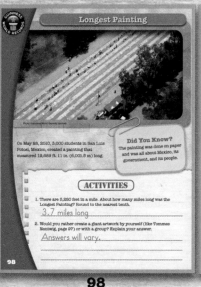

Joshua Mueller of Lakewood, Washington, has 403 different pairs of Converse shoes. He has been collecting them since 1991.

Did You Know?
The famous canvas and rubber shoes made by Converse are sometimes called Chuck Taylors, All Stars, Chucks, or Cons.

ACTIVITIES

1. If Mueller's shoe collection contained 31 different colors, how many pairs of each color would he have?
   13 pairs

2. If 285 pairs of the shoes were high-tops, how many pairs would be some other style?
   118 pairs

3. Is the state of Washington closer to the Atlantic Ocean or the Pacific Ocean?
   The Pacific Ocean

114

Tallest Bread Sculpture

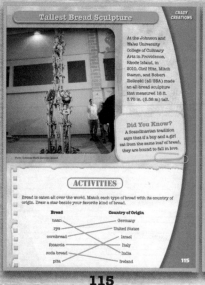

At the Johnson and Wales University College of Culinary Arts in Providence, Rhode Island, in 2010, Ciril Hitz, Mitch Stamm, and Robert Zolinski (all USA) made an all-bread sculpture that measured 18 ft. 2.75 in. (5.55 m) tall.

Did You Know?
A Scandinavian tradition says that if a boy and a girl eat from the same loaf of bread, they are bound to fall in love.

ACTIVITIES

Bread is eaten all over the world. Match each type of bread with its country of origin. Draw a star beside your favorite kind of bread.

Bread	Country of Origin
naan	Germany
rye	United States
cornbread	Israel
focaccia	Italy
soda bread	India
pita	Ireland

115

Largest Car Mosaic

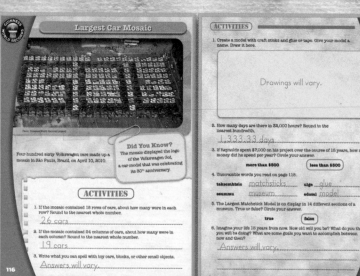

Four hundred sixty Volkswagen cars made up a mosaic in São Paulo, Brazil, on April 10, 2010.

Did You Know?
The mosaic displayed the logo of the Volkswagen Gol, a car model that was celebrating its 30th anniversary.

ACTIVITIES

1. If the mosaic contained 18 rows of cars, about how many were in each row? Round to the nearest whole number.
   26 cars

2. If the mosaic contained 24 columns of cars, about how many were in each column? Round to the nearest whole number.
   19 cars

3. Write what you can spell with toy cars, blocks, or other small objects.
   Answers will vary.

116

ACTIVITIES

1. Create a model with craft sticks and glue or tape. Give your model a name. Draw it here.

   Drawings will vary.

2. How many days are there in 32,000 hours? Round to the nearest hundredth.
   1,333.33 days

3. If Reynolds spent $7,000 on his project over the course of 15 years, how much money did he spend per year? Circle your answer.
   more than $500   less than $500

4. Unscramble words you read on page 118.
   takcsmhtsic matchsticks   ulge glue
   esumnu museum   edoml model

5. The Largest Matchstick Model is on display in 14 different sections of a museum. True or false? Circle your answer.
   true   false

6. Imagine your life 15 years from now. How old will you be? What do you think you will be doing? What are some goals you want to accomplish between now and then?
   Answers will vary.

119

Largest Sequin Mosaic

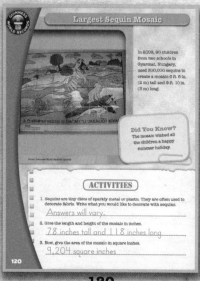

In 2009, 90 children from two schools in Gyaraspal, Hungary, used 200,000 sequins to create a mosaic 6 ft. 6 in. (2 m) tall and 9 ft. 10 in. (3 m) long.

Did You Know?
The mosaic wished all the children a happy summer holiday.

ACTIVITIES

1. Sequins are tiny discs of sparkly metal or plastic. They are often used to decorate fabric. Write what you would like to decorate with sequins.
   Answers will vary.

2. Give the length and height of the mosaic in inches.
   78 inches tall and 118 inches long

3. Now, give the area of the mosaic in square inches.
   9,204 square inches

120

Largest Wooden Sculpture

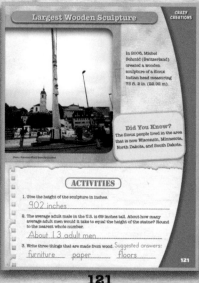

In 2005, Michel Schmid (Switzerland) created a wooden sculpture of a Sioux Indian head measuring 75 ft. 2 in. (22.92 m).

Did You Know?
The Sioux people lived in the area that is now Wisconsin, Minnesota, North Dakota, and South Dakota.

ACTIVITIES

1. Give the height of the sculpture in inches.
   902 inches

2. The average adult male in the U.S. is 69 inches tall. About how many average adult men would it take to equal the height of the statue? Round to the nearest whole number.
   About 13 adult men

3. Write three things that are made from wood. Suggested answers:
   furniture   paper   floors

121

Longest Drawing

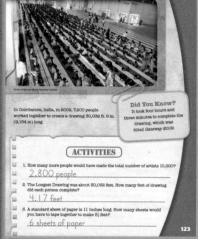

In Coimbatore, India, in 2009, 7,200 people worked together to create a drawing 30,032 ft. 9 in. (9,154 m) long.

Did You Know?
It took four hours and three minutes to complete the drawing, which was titled Gateway 2009.

ACTIVITIES

1. How many more people would have made the total number of artists 10,000?
   2,800 people

2. The Longest Drawing was about 30,032 feet. How many feet of drawing did each person complete?
   4.17 feet

3. A standard sheet of paper is 11 inches long. How many sheets would you have to tape together to make 5½ feet?
   6 sheets of paper

123

Largest Pushpin Mosaic

Over 10 months in 2008–2009, 210 members of the Junior Chamber International JB Entrepreneur in Malaysia used pushpins to create a mosaic 30 ft. 6 in. (9.35 m) by 21 ft. 11 in. (6.7 m).

Did You Know?
The mosaic was made up of 3.7 million pushpins.

ACTIVITIES

Unscramble names of school and office supplies.

neicip	pencil
huspnip	pushpin
lurer	ruler
palestr	stapler
luge	glue
rasemkr	markers

124

Longest Swim Under Ice (Breath Held)

Stig Åvall Severinsen (Denmark) swam 236 ft. 22 in. (72 m) under ice in Knudsø, Ry, Denmark, on March 6, 2010.

Did You Know?
The under-ice swim lasted for 86 seconds.

ACTIVITIES

1. Would you rather swim in water that is warm or cool? Explain your answer.
   Answers will vary.

2. If a swimming pool lap is 25 meters long, how many laps did Severinsen complete while swimming under ice?
   2.88 laps

3. Look at a map. Based on Denmark's location, do you think ice is commonly found there? Circle your answer.
   yes   no

126

Longest Garbage Truck Ramp Jump

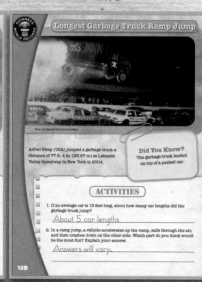

Alfred Sleep (USA) jumped a garbage truck a distance of 77 ft. 4 in. (23.57 m) at Lebanon Valley Speedway in New York in 2004.

Did You Know?
The garbage truck landed on top of a parked car.

ACTIVITIES

1. If an average car is 15 feet long, about how many car lengths did the garbage truck jump?
   About 5 car lengths

2. In a ramp jump, a vehicle accelerates up the ramp, sails through the air, and then crashes down on the other side. Which part do you think would be the most fun? Explain your answer.
   Answers will vary.

128

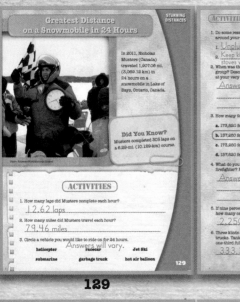

Greatest Distance on a Snowmobile in 24 Hours

STUNNING DISTANCES

In 2011, Nicholas Musters (Canada) traveled 1,907.06 mi. (3,069.12 km) in 24 hours on a snowmobile in Lake of Bays, Ontario, Canada.

Did You Know?
Musters completed 303 laps on a 6.29-mi. (10.189-km) course.

ACTIVITIES

1. How many laps did Musters complete each hour?
   12.62 laps

2. How many miles did Musters travel each hour?
   79.46 miles

3. Circle a vehicle you would like to ride on for 24 hours.
   Answers will vary.

   helicopter   racecar   Jet Ski
   submarine   garbage truck   hot air balloon

129

ACTIVITIES

STUNNING DISTANCES

1. Do some research on fire safety. What are two ways to prevent fires around your home? *Suggested answers:*
   1. Unplug all electrical items not in use
   2. Keep kitchen towels and oven mitts away from stoves while cooking

2. When was the last time you were in a competition with another person or group? Describe it. Did competing with another person push you to perform at your very best?
   Answers will vary.

3. How many feet are in 35 miles?
   a. 173,550 feet
   b. 187,250 feet
   c. 173,250 feet
   d. 187,520 feet

4. What do you want to be when you grow up? Do you think you would like to be a firefighter? Explain why or why not.
   Answers will vary.

5. If nine percent of the 25 million calls to fire departments were false alarms, how many calls were false alarms?
   2,250,000 calls

6. Three kinds of fire trucks are pumper trucks, ladder trucks, and tanker trucks. Tanker trucks can hold 1,000 gallons of water. If a tanker truck is one-third full, how much water does it carry?
   333.3 gallons

131

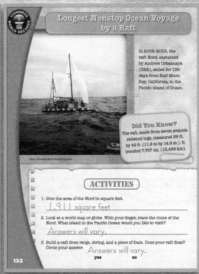

Longest Nonstop Ocean Voyage by a Raft

In 2002-2003, the raft *Nord*, captained by Andrew Urbanczyk (USA), sailed for 136 days from Half Moon Bay, California, to the Pacific island of Guam.

Did You Know?
The raft, made from seven sequoia redwood logs, measured 29 ft. by 49 ft. (11.9 m by 14.9 m). It traveled 7,767 mi. (12,499 km).

ACTIVITIES

1. Give the area of the *Nord* in square feet.
   1,911 square feet

2. Look at a world map or globe. With your finger, trace the route of the *Nord*. What island in the Pacific Ocean would you like to visit?
   Answers will vary.

3. Build a raft from twigs, string, and a piece of foam. Does your raft float? Circle your answer. Answers will vary.
   yes   no

132

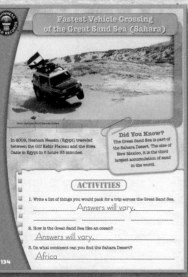

Fastest Vehicle Crossing of the Great Sand Sea (Sahara)

In 2009, Hesham Nessim (Egypt) traveled between the Gilf Kebir Plateau and the Siwa Oasis in Egypt in 8 hours 33 minutes.

Did You Know?
The Great Sand Sea is part of the Sahara Desert. The size of New Mexico, it is the third largest accumulation of sand in the world.

ACTIVITIES

1. Write a list of things you would pack for a trip across the Great Sand Sea.
   Answers will vary.

2. How is the Great Sand Sea like an ocean?
   Answers will vary.

3. On what continent can you find the Sahara Desert?
   Africa

134

Fastest Crossing of Canada on Foot (Female)

STUNNING DISTANCES

Over 143 days in 2002, Anne Keane (Canada) ran across Canada from St. John's, Newfoundland, to Tofino, British Columbia. She ran for 4,566 mi. (7,351 km).

Did You Know?
Keane ran for all but three of the 143 days.

ACTIVITIES

1. Circle the side of Canada on which Keane began her journey.
   east   west

2. Circle the side of Canada on which Keane ended her journey.
   east   west

3. What ocean did Keane see at the beginning of her journey? What ocean did she see at the end?
   At the beginning, the Atlantic Ocean; at the end, the Pacific Ocean

135

ACTIVITIES

STUNNING DISTANCES

1. There are 0.62 miles in one kilometer. How many miles are there in 100 kilometers? Circle your answer.
   more than 60 miles   less than 60 miles

2. How many more miles did Joachim run in 24 hours than Beroes?
   a. 6.64 miles
   b. 4.66 miles
   c. 60.24 miles
   d. 134.04 miles

3. Look at a map of your state. What city is about 150 miles away from where you live?
   Answers will vary.

4. Fill in vowel letters to complete words you read on page 136.
   u l t r a m a r a t h o n   r u n n e r

5. Circle the months that Beroes held the record for Greatest Distance Traveled on a Treadmill in 24 Hours by an Individual.

   January   May   September
   February   June   October
   March   July   November
   April   August   December

6. Would you want to be an ultramarathon runner? Explain why or why not.
   Answers will vary.

137

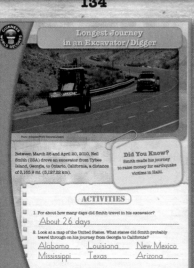

Longest Journey in an Excavator/Digger

Between March 26 and April 20, 2010, Neil Smith (USA) drove an excavator from Tybee Island, Georgia, to Ontario, California, a distance of 3,185.9 mi. (5,127.22 km).

Did You Know?
Smith made his journey to raise money for earthquake victims in Haiti.

ACTIVITIES

1. For about how many days did Smith travel in his excavator?
   About 26 days

2. Look at a map of the United States. What states did Smith probably travel through on his journey from Georgia to California?
   Alabama   Louisiana   New Mexico
   Mississippi   Texas   Arizona

140

ACTIVITIES

STUNNING DISTANCES

1. Find the Adriatic Sea on a map. Name two countries it borders.
   1. Suggested answer: Italy
   2. Suggested answer: Croatia

2. If Roguski swam 140 miles in 50 hours, what was his average speed in miles per hour? Round to the nearest tenth.
   a. 35 mph
   b. 0.4 mph
   c. 2.8 mph
   d. 3 mph

3. Circle five words you read on page 142 to complete the word search. Use the word bank to help you.

   ocean swim Italy Croatia wakeboard

C	R	O	A	T	I	A	X	W
M	V	O	A	E	P	C	O	A
W	W	E	K	M	G	X	E	K
O	I	D	O	W	A	O	8	E
O	P	I	V	G	W	C	W	B
U	E	T	Y	Z	E	E	I	O
K	R	A	H	U	W	A	M	A
J	F	T	I	L	Y	N	C	R
F	T	Y	M	P	T	A	Q	D

4. Do you know how to swim? How long can you swim without stopping or touching the ground? Ask an adult to time you.
   Answers will vary.

143

Most Vertical Distance Down a Fireman's Pole in One Hour by a Team of 10

STUNNING DISTANCES

A team of 10 firefighters (UK) slid down a fireman's pole a total of 17,191 ft. (5,240 m) in one hour in Hove, United Kingdom, on August 23, 2009.

Did You Know?
Many firefighters have a college degree in fire science.

ACTIVITIES

1. There are 5,280 feet in a mile. How many miles did the team of firefighters slide?
   3.25 miles

2. Some firefighters get injured sliding down poles. Many new stations have stairs or slides instead of poles. What do you think is the fastest way to go down: stairs, a slide, or a pole? Explain your answer.
   Answers will vary.

147

149

1. Why was the road sealed off for Al-Mamari's world record attempt? Do you think that was a good idea? Explain why or why not.
   Answers will vary.

2. What does it mean if two roads are parallel?
   a. The roads extend in the same direction, but never run into each other.
   b. The roads intersect at 90 degree angles.
   c. The roads cross over each other at least four times.
   d. One road circles the other.

3. How many miles did Al-Mamari travel per hour? Round to the nearest hundredth.
   55.07 miles per hour

4. Name three countries Oman borders.
   1. United Arab Emirates
   2. Saudi Arabia
   3. Yemen

5. Name a place you have traveled that is about 92 miles away from home. Ask an adult if you need help.
   Answers will vary.

6. How do you think Al-Mamari reacted after being one of the first people from Oman to set a Guinness World Record? Use three adjectives to describe how he might have felt. Suggested answers:
   proud   excited   victorious

149

151

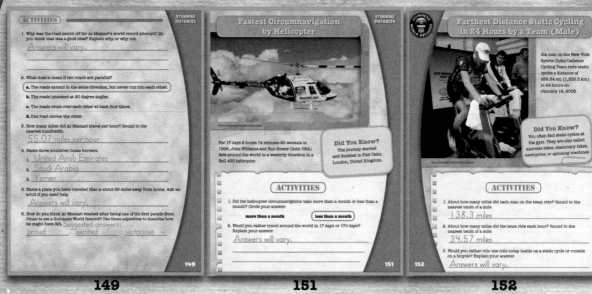

Fastest Circumnavigation by Helicopter

For 17 days 6 hours 14 minutes 25 seconds in 1996, John Williams and Ron Bower (both USA) flew around the world in a westerly direction in a Bell 430 helicopter.

Did You Know?
The journey started and finished in Fair Oaks, London, United Kingdom.

ACTIVITIES

1. Did the helicopter circumnavigation take more than a month or less than a month? Circle your answer.
   more than a month   **less than a month**

2. Would you rather travel around the world in 17 days or 170 days? Explain your answer.
   Answers will vary.

151

152

Farthest Distance Static Cycling in 24 Hours by a Team (Male)

Six men on the New York Sports Clubs/Cadence Cycling Team rode static cycles a distance of 829.84 mi. (1,335.5 km) in 24 hours on January 19, 2008.

Did You Know?
You often find static cycles at the gym. They are also called exercise bikes, stationary bikes, exercycles, or spinning machines.

ACTIVITIES

1. About how many miles did each man on the team ride? Round to the nearest tenth of a mile.
   138.3 miles

2. About how many miles did the team ride each hour? Round to the nearest tenth of a mile.
   34.57 miles

3. Would you rather ride one mile today inside on a static cycle or outside on a bicycle? Explain your answer.
   Answers will vary.

152

153

Longest Marathon on a Fairground/Theme Park Attraction

The longest marathon on a traditional fairground attraction lasted 24 hours 30 minutes and was achieved by Brenda Donohue (Ireland) at The Point Village, Dublin, Ireland, on October 23, 2011.

Did You Know?
Donohue rode on a Ferris wheel.

ACTIVITIES

1. The first Ferris wheel was erected in Chicago in 1893. The giant wheel had 36 huge gondolas that could each seat 40 riders. How many people could ride the wheel at once?
   1,440 people

2. Engineer George Ferris invented the Ferris wheel during the late 19th century. Circle the names of other marvels invented around this same time.
   personal computers   trains   **electric lights**
   smart phones   space shuttles   **telephones**

153

155

1. Look at this map of the United States. Color the 18 states Spencer may have ridden through during his world record journey.

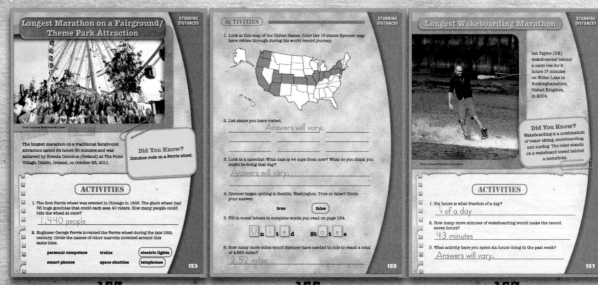

2. List states you have visited.
   Answers will vary.

3. Look at a calendar. What date is 44 days from now? What do you think you might be doing that day?
   Answers will vary.

4. Spencer began cycling in Seattle, Washington. True or false? Circle your answer.
   true   false

5. Fill in vowel letters to complete words you read on page 154.
   U n i t e d   S t a t e s

6. How many more miles would Spencer have needed to ride to reach a total of 4,666 miles?
   2.52 miles

155

157

Longest Wakeboarding Marathon

Ian Taylor (UK) wakeboarded behind a cable tow for 6 hours 17 minutes on Willen Lake in Buckinghamshire, United Kingdom, in 2004.

Did You Know?
Wakeboarding is a combination of water skiing, snowboarding, and surfing. The rider stands on a wakeboard towed behind a motorboat.

ACTIVITIES

1. Six hours is what fraction of a day?
   ¼ of a day

2. How many more minutes of wakeboarding would make the record seven hours?
   43 minutes

3. What activity have you spent six hours doing in the past week?
   Answers will vary.

157

158

Farthest Distance Nordic Walking in 24 Hours

Walter Geckle (Austria) used Nordic walking to travel a distance of 108.74 mi. (175 km) in 24 hours in Dienmark, Austria, in 2010.

Did You Know?
In Nordic walking, a walker uses poles similar to ski poles. The sport is also called ski walking. It provides a full-body workout.

ACTIVITIES

1. Nordic walking can be enjoyed year-round. What is your favorite sport or exercise to do in any season?
   Answers will vary.

2. How many miles did Geckle walk each hour? Round to the nearest tenth of a mile.
   4.53 miles

3. Name another sport that requires you to hold some type of pole or stick.
   Answers will vary.

158

161

1. Complete the crossword puzzle with words you read on page 160.

Across
2. Guenci traveled 24.004 of these in one hour
5. Guenci's first name
6. Inline skates are _____ than traditional skates.
7. _____ have two to five wheels in a single line.
8. Guenci set his world record on a _____.

Down
1. Inline skates are a type of _____.
3. Guenci is from _____.
4. Guenci's profession

Crossword answers:
- ROLLERSKATE
- MILES
- ITALY
- MAURO
- FASTER
- FLIGHT
- INLINESKATES
- TRACK

2. What was Guenci's average speed in miles per hour?
   24.004 mph

3. Do you like to roller skate? Explain why or why not.
   Answers will vary.

161

162

Longest Paddleboard Journey (Team)

Three French women (Stephanie Geyer-Barneix, Alexandra Lux, and Flora Manciet) used their hands to paddleboard 3,001 mi. (4,830 km) from Cape Breton, Canada, to Capbreton, France, in 2009.

Did You Know?
The paddleboard journey took 54 days.

ACTIVITIES

1. Did the paddleboard trip take closer to one month or closer to two months? Circle your answer.
   one month   **two months**

2. The women paddled from the east coast of Canada to the west coast of France. Which ocean did they cross?
   The Atlantic Ocean

3. Would you rather paddleboard alone or as a member of a team?
   Answers will vary.

162

Longest Journey on a Motorized Bicycle

STUNNING DISTANCES

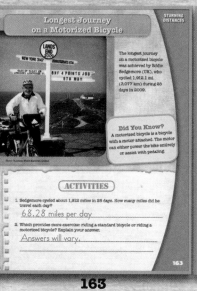

The longest journey on a motorized bicycle was achieved by Eddie Sedgemore (UK), who cycled 1,912.1 mi. (3,077 km) during 28 days in 2009.

Did You Know?
A motorized bicycle is a bicycle with a motor attached. The motor can either power the bike entirely or assist with pedaling.

ACTIVITIES

1. Sedgemore cycled about 1,912 miles in 28 days. How many miles did he travel each day?
   68.28 miles per day

2. Which provides more exercise: riding a standard bicycle or riding a motorized bicycle? Explain your answer.
   Answers will vary.

163

163

Fastest 100 Meters on a Space Hopper (Male)

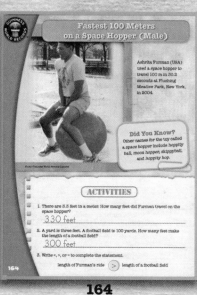

Ashrita Furman (USA) used a space hopper to travel 100 m in 30.2 seconds at Flushing Meadow Park, New York, in 2004.

Did You Know?
Other names for the toy called a space hopper include hoppity ball, moon hopper, skippyball, and hoppity hop.

ACTIVITIES

1. There are 3.3 feet in a meter. How many feet did Furman travel on the space hopper?
   330 feet

2. A yard is three feet. A football field is 100 yards. How many feet make the length of a football field?
   300 feet

3. Write <, >, or = to complete the statement.
   length of Furman's ride > length of a football field

164

164

Farthest Distance Static Cycling in 24 Hours by a Team (Female)

STUNNING DISTANCES

Six women on Team GanCare (South Africa) static cycled 722.03 mi. (1,162 km) in 24 hours on November 4–5, 2010, in Honeydew, South Africa.

Did You Know?
A recumbent cycle allows the rider to lean back in a lying position.

ACTIVITIES

1. Who achieved a world record first—the women's static cycling team or the men's static cycling team (page 162)?
   The men's team

2. How many more miles did the men's team ride than the women's team?
   107.81 miles

3. How many official languages are spoken in South Africa? Do some research to find out.
   11 languages

165

165

ACTIVITIES

STUNNING DISTANCES

1. If you were to ride a motorcycle around the world, what are the top five countries you would most like to visit?
   1. _____ 4. Answers will vary.
   2. _____ 5. _____
   3. _____

2. Finish the sentence.
   Pulko took over 35,000 pictures on her journey.

3. How many days are in five years? How many days are in six years?
   1,825 days; 2,190 days

4. If Pulko spent $100,000 over five and a half years, how much did she spend per year? Round to the nearest penny.
   a. $18,181
   b. $18,181.82
   c. $20,000
   d. $16,384.62

5. List the continents that Pulko drove through on her motorcycle journey.
   1. North America 5. Europe
   2. South America 6. Africa
   3. Antarctica   7. Australia
   4. Asia

6. What do you think was the most exciting thing Pulko encountered on her trip around the world?
   Answers will vary.

167

167

Longest Solo Row Across an Ocean

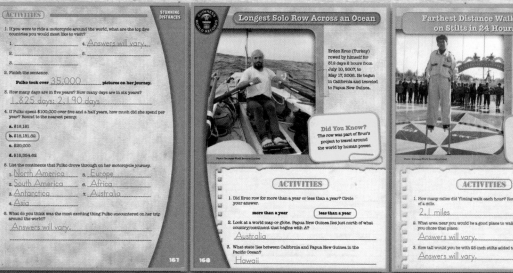

Erden Eruc (Turkey) rowed by himself for 312 days 2 hours from July 10, 2007, to May 17, 2008. He began in California and traveled to Papua New Guinea.

Did You Know?
The row was part of Eruc's project to travel around the world by human power.

ACTIVITIES

1. Did Eruc row for more than a year or less than a year? Circle your answer.
   more than a year   less than a year

2. Look at a world map or globe. Papua New Guinea lies just north of what country/continent that begins with A?
   Australia

3. What state lies between California and Papua New Guinea in the Pacific Ocean?
   Hawaii

168

168

Farthest Distance Walking on Stilts in 24 Hours

STUNNING DISTANCES

In 24 hours, Saimaiti Yiming (China) walked on stilts 49.4 mi. (79.6 km) around Shanshan County, Xinjiang, China, in 2003.

Did You Know?
Yiming's stilts measured 28.7 in. (73 cm) from the ground to his ankle.

ACTIVITIES

1. How many miles did Yiming walk each hour? Round to the nearest tenth of a mile.
   2.1 miles

2. What area near you would be a good place to walk on stilts? Explain why you chose that place.
   Answers will vary.

3. How tall would you be with 28-inch stilts added to your height?
   Answers will vary.

169

169

Longest Snowboarding Marathon

STUNNING DISTANCES

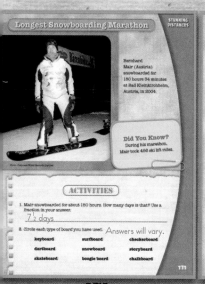

Bernhard Mair (Austria) snowboarded for 180 hours 34 minutes at Bad Kleinkirchheim, Austria, in 2004.

Did You Know?
During his marathon, Mair took 456 ski lift rides.

ACTIVITIES

1. Mair snowboarded for about 180 hours. How many days is that? Use a fraction in your answer.
   7½ days

2. Circle each type of board you have used. Answers will vary.
   keyboard   surfboard   checkerboard
   dartboard   snowboard   storyboard
   skateboard   boogie board chalkboard

171

171

ACTIVITIES

STUNNING DISTANCES

1. If Parry had raised $5 per mile for charity on his 24-hour journey, how much money would he have raised?
   a. $505
   b. $120
   c. $23,280
   d. $300

2. What would be the advantages of driving a motorized scooter versus a car? What would be the disadvantages?
   Advantages: Suggested answer: You would get better gas mileage.
   Disadvantages: Suggested answer: You couldn't drive as fast.

3. How many months ago did Parry set the record for Greatest Distance by Scooter in 24 Hours?
   Answers will vary depending on the current month and year.

4. What do you want to do after you graduate high school?
   Answers will vary.

5. Imagine that you want to raise money for charity by setting a world record. How would you raise donations? Create a poster advertising your world record and asking people to sponsor you on your attempt.

   Posters will vary.

173

173

Farthest Distance Traveled on a Unicycle in 24 Hours

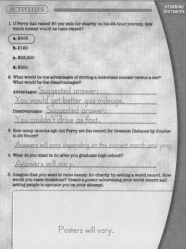

Sam Wakeling (UK) covered 281.85 mi. (453.6 km) on a unicycle in 24 hours at Aberystwyth, Wales, United Kingdom, in 2007.

Did You Know?
Most unicycles have no gears or chains. The pedals directly crank the axle and move the wheel.

ACTIVITIES

1. How many miles did Wakeling ride each hour?
   11.74 miles

2. Wakeling set his record in 2007. How many years ago was that?
   Answers will vary.

3. Learning to ride a unicycle requires many hours of practice. What have you spent many hours practicing?
   Answers will vary.

174

174

Fastest True Circumnavigation by Bicycle (Male)

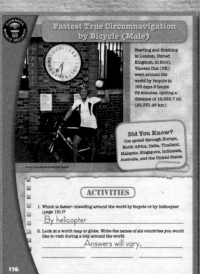

Starting and finishing in London, United Kingdom, in 2010, Vincent Cox (UK) went around the world by bicycle in 163 days 6 hours 58 minutes, cycling a distance of 18,225.7 mi. (29,331.45 km).

Did You Know?
Cox cycled through Europe, North Africa, India, Thailand, Malaysia, Singapore, Indonesia, Australia, and the United States.

ACTIVITIES

1. Which is faster—traveling around the world by bicycle or by helicopter (page 151)?
   By helicopter

2. Look at a world map or globe. Write the names of six countries you would like to visit during a trip around the world.
   Answers will vary.

176

Farthest Distance by Canoe/Kayak on Flat Water in 24 Hours (Female)

STUNNING DISTANCES

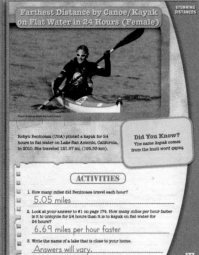

Robyn Benincasa (USA) piloted a kayak for 24 hours in flat water on Lake San Antonio, California, in 2010. She traveled 121.37 mi. (195.33 km).

Did You Know?
The name *kayak* comes from the Inuit word *qayaq*.

ACTIVITIES

1. How many miles did Benincasa travel each hour?
   5.05 miles

2. Look at your answer to #1 on page 174. How many miles per hour faster is it to unicycle for 24 hours than it is to kayak on flat water for 24 hours?
   6.69 miles per hour faster

3. Write the name of a lake that is close to your home.
   Answers will vary.

177

ACTIVITIES

STUNNING DISTANCES

1. Do you think static cycling is a good form of exercise? Explain why or why not.
   Answers will vary.

2. In Müller's 12-hour world record, what was her average speed in miles per hour? Round to the nearest tenth.
   a. 8.4 mph
   b. 8.8 mph
   c. 17.5 mph
   d. 16.8 mph

3. Look at your answer to #2. Was Müller's average distance in miles per hour over the course of her 12-hour record more or less than the distance she cycled for her one-hour world record? Circle your answer.
   more   (less)

4. What is your favorite way to exercise?
   Answers will vary.

5. Circle five words you read on page 178 to complete the word search. Use the word bank to help you.

   `biking running yoga basketball weights`

I	R	H	M	J	B	A	F	B	H
P	U	V	S	D	U	R	H	A	Y
V	N	U	I	E	T	R	G	S	K
R	A	N	U	L	E	E	W	K	W
A	I	P	U	L	E	F	R	E	E
A	N	Z	X	V	O	L	V	T	I
Y	G	S	P	B	Y	G	M	B	G
O	Q	(B	I	K	I	N	G)	A	H
G	B	V	O	I	E	Y	Q	X	T
A	A	W	A	V	D	G	G	L	S

179

Greatest Karting Distance in 24 Hours Outdoors (Individual)

STUNNING DISTANCES

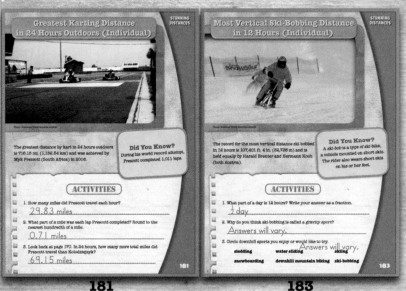

The greatest distance by kart in 24 hours outdoors is 716.18 mi. (1,152.54 km) and was achieved by Myk Prescott (South Africa) in 2005.

Did You Know?
During his world record attempt, Prescott completed 1,011 laps.

ACTIVITIES

1. How many miles did Prescott travel each hour?
   29.83 miles

2. What part of a mile was each lap Prescott completed? Round to the nearest hundredth of a mile.
   0.71 miles

3. Look back at page 170. In 24 hours, how many more total miles did Prescott travel than Kolodziejczyk?
   69.15 miles

181

Most Vertical Ski-Bobbing Distance in 12 Hours (Individual)

STUNNING DISTANCES

The record for the most vertical distance ski-bobbed in 12 hours is 107,401 ft. 4 in. (32,736 m) and is held equally by Harald Brenter and Hermann Koch (both Austria).

Did You Know?
A ski-bob is a type of ski-bike, a vehicle mounted on short skis. The rider also wears short skis on his or her feet.

ACTIVITIES

1. What part of a day is 12 hours? Write your answer as a fraction.
   $\frac{1}{2}$ day

2. Why do you think ski-bobbing is called a gravity sport?
   Answers will vary.

3. Circle downhill sports you enjoy or would like to try.   Answers will vary.
   sledding   water sliding   skiing
   snowboarding   downhill mountain biking   ski-bobbing

183

196